Our School:
Calvin College and the Christian Reformed Church

Harry Boonstra

255 Jefferson Ave., S.E., Grand Rapids, Mich., 49503

Printed in the United States of America

ISBN 0-8028-3950-9

The Historical Series of the Reformed Church in America

No. 39

Our School:
Calvin College and the Christian Reformed Church

Harry Boonstra

Wm. B. Eerdmans Publishing Co.
Grand Rapids, Michigan

The Historical Series of the Reformed Church in America

This series has been inaugurated by the General Synod of the Reformed Church in America, acting through its Commission on History, for the purpose of encouraging historical research and providing a medium wherein this knowledge may be shared with the academic community and with the members of the denomination in order that a knowledge of the past may contribute to right action in the present.

Contents

Editor's Preface

When the historical series of the Reformed Church in America publishes a book entitled *Our School*, our readers expect it to be about Hope, Central, or Northwestern College. The surprise (especially for basketball fans) comes in the subtitle, *Calvin College and the Christian Reformed Church*. However, for those who have been following the gradually widening cooperation between the Reformed and Christian Reformed churches, this volume will be seen as little more than one event in a series.

As early as 1963, Willard Wichers, Gerrit ten Zyhthof, John Kromminga and Lester DeKoster helped bring to fruition the Dutch American Historical Committee, composed of Calvin College, Calvin Seminary, Hope College, Western Seminary, and the City of Holland for the purpose of sharing access to their respective archival holdings. That endeavor proved so successful that it has broadened into the publication of such historical works as Henry S. Lucas's *Netherlanders in America*, and soon, as part of this historical series, *Amsterdamse Emigranten*, by Dr. J. Stellingwerff.

More recently, beginning in the early 1980s, the two denominations have cooperated in the production of church, school, and catechetical materials published by CRC Publications. In 1991, two prestigious publications, the *Reformed Journal* (published by Eerdmans, but effectively a voice of the Christian Reformed Church) and *Perspectives*, a journal of the RCA, joined forces with a board composed of representatives of both communions. It now publishes under the name, *Perspectives*.

On the classical and congregational levels, committees composed of representatives of both denominations have urged both pulpit exchanges and joint services. In the classes of Holland, Michigan, Reformed and Christian Reformed, the third millennium began auspiciously with a joint service held in Hope College's Dimnent Chapel. The Reverend Stan Mast of LaGrave Avenue Christian Reformed preached, and the Reverends Kama Jongerius of Third Reformed and Marvin Hoffman of Fourteenth Street CRC officiated at the Lord's Table, one consecrating the bread and the other the wine, with the congregation of Reformed and Christian Reformed church members coming forward to partake.

While the Reformed Church in America has no publication equal to *Origins* (which publishes articles on immigration and on the educational institutions of the two communions), neither does the Christian Reformed Church have a historical series equivalent to that of the RCA. Therefore, the publication of *Our School* is but one more example of the mutually beneficial cooperation of those who share the Reformed faith.

However, in addition to being one more evidence of cooperation between the two denominations, *Our School* is an important document to help members of the Reformed Church in America better understand the Christian Reformed Church. This is especially so for those church leaders who are newcomers to the RCA. Proposals for further cooperation and closer union are sure to come. Some actions, past and present, of the Christian Reformed Church will be seen as negative factors. Others will certainly be seen as positive. A reading of this volume will present both and thus contribute to a more complete understanding of our sister denomination. With such understanding, our two denominations can continue to fulfill the mandate of our Lord to love, and to draw closer together that in him all may be one.

Donald J. Bruggink
General Editor

Preface

The history of Calvin College is a fascinating one, and I have thoroughly enjoyed the opportunity to delve into it. The contribution of the college, as well as the lives of its students and faculty, make for interesting research. However, this work is not intended to be a full-fledged history of Calvin College. Such a history would include topics such as the success of the hockey team or the increase in faculty salaries. I will discuss neither.

Rather, my focus will be on the interaction, the mutual influence between Calvin College and the Christian Reformed Church. This interaction obviously comes into play in the origin of the college but will be seen also in much of its subsequent history. Curriculum, student conduct, student publications, faculty hiring (and occasional firing), faculty views, and a host of other issues were and are affected by the relationship between the college and the church.

In tracing this history I have had to consider many areas and disciplines. The history of the relationship between the church and the college involves various issues in theology (Sabbath observance, interpretation of Genesis, common grace), philosophy, anthropology, geology, astronomy, film, drama, music, and card playing. I obviously do not claim to be an expert in all these fields (least of all card playing). I have relied on many guides in entering these disciplines and have tried to present the areas as fairly as possible and as completely as necessary.

The "completely as necessary" was always guided by the theme: how does this issue portray or illuminate the relationship between Calvin College and the Christian Reformed Church? For example, the debate on creation and evolution deserves a full-length treatment, delineating and interpreting the many theological and scientific questions. I will not even come close to such treatment, and the reader will look in vain, for example, for an exposition on Creation Science. Rather, I explore this issue only in the context of the relationship (conflict) between college and church.

A constant question during the writing was, "How do I fairly balance the church's criticism of the college with the long history of mutual benefit and appreciation?" In terms of space devoted to various issues, the criticism and censure loom much larger than the approval. In various chapters I have explained why my emphasis is often on the tension between church and school. Put briefly, it was mostly during and after the controversies that church and college defined and redefined their relationship. However, I hope that I have also repeated often enough that this tension must always be seen in the context of a century and more of concord. Another question concerns the issues and topics selected. I do not deal with every issue that arose between college and church. Rather, I have chosen a number of issues that exemplify and demonstrate the relationship.

I have had various readers in mind while writing the book. Students and alumni of Calvin will recognize at least part of their college experience and perhaps have moments of "so that's what was going on," when reflecting on their education. New faculty not acquainted with Calvin will be able to understand the (sub)culture of Calvin College better when seeing some of its history and its relation to its mother denomination. Scholars in Christian colleges and those who study higher education will see part of the mosaic that makes up Christian higher education. Those interested in the Christian Reformed Church will discern better the history and nature of that denomination.

My research has made use of the standard tools of books, journals, magazines, conference papers, and other resources. In addition, I have often relied on the *Acts of Synod of the Christian Reformed Church*. Perhaps most importantly, I have had full access (except for restricted material) to the Calvin Heritage Hall Archives. Reports, proposals, minutes, and correspondence of faculty, committees, administration, and trustees have been an invaluable resource. I am deeply indebted to Richard Harms, director of Heritage Hall, and his staff, for their unfailing help and for the use of a research office. Readers of earlier drafts included Elton Bruins, Conrad Bult, Joel Carpenter, James De Jong, Richard Harms, George Marsden, William Spoelhof, Henrietta Ten Harmsel, Jeff Tyler, and Henry Zwaanstra. In various ways their critiques helped sharpen my focus and improve my grasp of the history. My occasional stubbornness in not heeding their advice is hardly their fault. Donald Bruggink was a perceptive editor, always finding the right balance between critique and encouragement.

Writing this study in the year of the 125th anniversary of Calvin College and Seminary was especially meaningful, since it afforded the opportunity to reflect on the great blessings bestowed on school and church.

Harry Boonstra
Spring, 2001

1
Introduction: Calvin as a Church College

A question that suggests the theme of this chapter might well be, "What do Abraham Kuyper, Father Theodore Hesburgh, Bob Jones, and Gaylen Byker have in common?" The proper answer would be, "They all wrote about the relationship between the Christian faith and education, and they each headed a Christian college or university." Of course, besides their commonality, there is also great disparity among the foursome; that disparity indicates the wide variety of proposed solutions to the relationship between faith and reason and the greatly different academic institutions that they and others represent. Even though this study deals with one college and one denomination, in this introduction I will suggest that the issues and questions that arose between Calvin College and the Christian Reformed Church (CRC) are also found in the issues and stories of other schools and other traditions. At the same time, we will see that in some significant ways Calvin is different from other Christian colleges. Placing the Calvin College chronicle in the context of Christian higher education (be it Reformed, Roman Catholic, or Fundamentalist) will help us understand the Calvin-CRC dynamics better. (Readers who want to get to "the real story" of this book may want to begin at chapter 2. However, this chapter will help in grasping many of the issues in the Calvin College history).

Denominational and/or Christian colleges and universities have been on the North American scene virtually from the beginning of European settlements, and a rationale for those schools was often carefully articulated. At the founding of Wellesley College, for instance, the founders summed up succinctly, "The Institution will be Christian in its influence, discipline, and course of instruction." In more recent times, a deliberate attempt to answer the question about the relationship between faith and learning has come to the fore, especially since 1950.[1]

Integration of Faith and Learning

Perhaps the most important issue in Christian (higher) education can be framed as this question: "How is the Christian faith related

[1] One of the earlier efforts was presented in the first Danforth Lectures by Nels F.S. Ferre, later published in book form as *Christian Faith and Higher Education* (New York: Harper, 1954). Since then a large number of essays, conferences, dissertations, collections, and monographs have been written. Among the better known are William C. Ringenberg, *The Christian College: A History of Protestant Higher Education in America* (Grand Rapids: Eerdmans, 1984) and Arthur Holmes, *The Idea of a Christian College* (Grand Rapids: Eerdmans, 1975, 1987). Most comprehensive and most widely quoted are George Marsden's *The Soul of the American University* (New York: Oxford, 1994) and *The Outrageous Idea of Christian Scholarship*, (New York: Oxford, 1997) . Much reviewed recently was James T. Burtchaell, *The Dying of the Light: The Disengagement of Colleges and Universities from their Christian Churches* (Grand Rapids: Eerdmans, 1998). More theological, but also extensively quoted was Pope John Paul's encyclical letter, *Faith and Reason*, (1998). Helpful anthologies are: Robert Rue Parsonage, ed., *Church Related Higher Education*, (Valley Forge, PA: Judson Press, 1978); Joel Carpenter and Kenneth Shipps, eds., *Making Higher Education Christian: The History and Mission of Evangelical Colleges in America* (Grand Rapids: Eerdmans, 1987); Harold Heie and David Wolfe, eds., *The Reality of Christian Learning: Strategies for Faith-Discipline Integration* (Grand Rapids: Eerdmans, 1987); Richard Hughes and William Adrian, eds., *Models for Christian Higher Education* (Grand Rapids: Eerdmans, 1997); David Dockery and David Gushe, eds., *The Future of Christian Higher Education* (Nashville: Broadman, 1999). A recent title with a somewhat different focus but also pertinent here is Anthony J. Diekema, *Academic Freedom & Christian Scholarship* (Grand Rapids: Eerdmans, 2000). Each of these titles contains yet more bibliographies. I will return to Marsden and Diekema in my final chapter.

to learning and scholarship?" The question finds expression in many different ways: How does theology influence sociology? Does Christianity have anything to say to or about astronomy? Is there a Christian geometry? Why the need for journals such as *Christianity and Literature, Christianity and Society, Religion and Culture, Christian Scholars Review*?

The answers have been as numerous as the questions, and hundreds of Christian colleges all practice some version of the faith-learning relationship. The Hillsdale College catalog, for example, is rather anemic in its acknowledgment that both the college and each student are to be "a trustee of modern man's intellectual and spiritual inheritance from the Judeo-Christian faith." Near the other end of the spectrum is Bob Jones University, which states explicitly that each student "can be certain that every aspect of University life has Christ at its center, and the Bible as its foundation." It is "a place that will provide an environment to saturate him with the ways and will of God." Hope College "is...affiliated with the Reformed Church in America. Its great religious heritage is expressed through a dynamic Christian community of students and teachers vitally concerned with a relevant faith that changes lives and transforms society." Thus the various catalogs try to encapsulate the vision and mission of each college.

The spectrum of responses is highlighted in James Estep's essay, "Faith as the Transformation of Learning."[2] Here he uses Richard Niebuhr's famous *Christ and Culture* to chart the various ways in which Christian scholars and institutions have worked out a relationship between their faith and scholarship. Faith and learning may be (1) in a dualistic relationship, exhibiting especially the tension between the two areas; or (2) in synthesis, tending to a merger of faith and learning; or (3) in conversion, with areas of disagreements either adapted or rejected. Estep's analysis demonstrates the many creative avenues that Christian scholars

2 *Christian Education Journal*, 2NS (1998), 59-76.

have explored to articulate the interaction between the Christian faith and academic disciplines.

Calvin College's Contribution

Even though many minds have dealt with this issue, various Christian traditions have formulated careful answers, and numerous Christian colleges have shaped their curricula according to a faith-and-learning pattern, one can also claim that Calvin College has occupied an important place in this discussion.

One reason for such importance is, no doubt, the Dutch Reformed inheritance, especially as embodied in Abraham Kuyper. (See also chapter 2 and other sections for references to Kuyper). In one of his most famous lectures, delivered at the founding of the (Calvinistic) Free University in Amsterdam, Kuyper emphasized that all of life and all of culture "belong" to Christ and are to be claimed by the Christian scholar. Kuyper's motto has been repeated as a slogan by many Dutch Calvinists (and American evangelicals!) ever since: "There is not an inch in the whole estate of our human existence, of which Christ, who is Sovereign over all, does not proclaim: 'It is Mine!'"[3] This motto did not spell out exactly how faith and learning were to be related, but it did validate the scholar's entry into every academic field, not just to enlarge the knowledge of a discipline, but also to bring the Christian faith to bear on that knowledge.

Henry Ryskamp, academic dean at Calvin for many years, recalls that faculty discussions in 1918 about the emerging four-year curriculum included the question, "Does the new curriculum under discussion and the faculty available for the teaching of it make it possible for us to teach and develop the principles of Reformed truth so as to serve these students, not only with the necessary subjects, but also with those which make for the further development and integration of a Christian view of life?"[4] Writing two years after

3 Abraham Kuyper, *Souvereiniteit in Eigen Kring* (Amsterdam: Kruyt, 1880), 35.

4 Henry J. Ryskamp, *Offering Hearts, Shaping Lives: A History of Calvin College 1876-1966* (Grand Rapids: Calvin College, 2000), 63.

the first class graduated from Calvin College, theologian Louis Berkhof drew on both John Calvin and Abraham Kuyper when he wrote: "The great task to which [the college] is expected to address itself, is to apply these principles in every field of study, as the nature of the case may demand, and to exhibit their bearing on life in all its phases....Only a consistent application of our Reformed principles to every branch of study, making the instruction at our School thoroughly distinctive, can satisfy."[5] Such lofty goals were not always achieved; indeed many of the criticisms of the college voiced later assailed Calvin for its failures in these goals. However, it is significant that from its founding, the principle of (somehow) integrating the Christian faith with all learning and scholarship was deemed essential.

This desire for integration did not mean, however, that the curriculum as such was particularly indebted to a Calvinistic tradition—other than that the pre-seminary program included a course in Calvinism and in Dutch History! (*Year Book*, 1923-1924). The initial collection of courses was little more than a compilation of courses commonly taught in American colleges—modeled largely on the curriculum of the undergraduate program at the University of Michigan. Fundamental questions about the curriculum came later. In 1958 W. Harry Jellema, Calvin College philosophy professor, published a serious scrutiny of the curriculum, "The Curriculum in a Liberal Arts College." Though generally ignored, both at Calvin and elsewhere, the booklet was significant in critiquing the curriculum of Calvin College up to that time, as well as the curricula of most other Christian colleges. Jellema was especially intent on pressing the claims of liberal arts and classical studies, but he also suggested the contours of a Christian mind in such studies.

[5] Louis Berkhof, "Our School's Reason for Existence and the Preservation Thereof," in *Semi-Centennial Volume, Theological School and Calvin College* (Grand Rapids: Calvin College, 1926), 131-32.

More thorough revision came in the document, *Christian Liberal Arts Education.* In 1963 president William Spoelhof had appointed a curriculum committee. This committee submitted a lengthy report in 1965, which was discussed thoroughly, modified, and accepted by the faculty.[6] A very important section of the report is "Faith and Learning" (pp. 57-61), in which the document sums up some of the most significant ways in which Christian belief governs scholarship and teaching. *Christian Liberal Arts Education* also travels from theoretical discussions ("Foundations of Christian Liberal Arts Education") to practical applications in terms of course sequences and college calendar ("Curriculum of a Christian Liberal Arts Education"). Although the two sections are integrally related, those outside of Calvin College have found the first part the most germane, since it could be applied to other colleges and various curricula.

Calvin College's contribution to Christian higher education has been recognized in other circles. In the Council for Christian Colleges and Universities (formerly Christian College Coalition), Calvin has always assumed a position of leadership. Current and former Calvin scholars regularly contribute essays to conferences and book collections on the foundations of Christian education, and their works are widely cited. Probably the most significant voice has been that of philosopher Nicholas Wolterstorff, who has authored both theoretical and "applied" contributions. His *Reason Within the Bounds of Religion* (1976; 2nd ed., 1984) has been especially influential in setting forth a masterful defense of Christian scholarship.

Let me cite four sources where these contributions have been recognized. William Ringenberg acknowledges: "One of the earliest institutional leaders of the integration emphasis was Calvin, the Christian Reformed college which has been influenced greatly by Abraham Kuyper...."[7] In his introduction to *Models for Christian*

[6] Published as a monograph by Eerdmans in 1970.
[7] Ringenberg, *Christian College,* 199.

Education, Richard Hughes indirectly identifies Calvin College as a leader: "Several scholars from the Reformed tradition currently stand at the cutting edge of discussions regarding Christian higher education and urge the rest of us to employ a 'Christian worldview' in our work as well."[8] Hughes then specifically mentions George Marsden, Nicholas Wolterstorff, and Ronald Wells. (In the next sentence Hughes cautions that these Reformed folk are not the only ones who have made important contributions, and points to Mennonite, Lutheran, and Catholic sources.) James C. Turner, a University of Notre Dame scholar, hands out even more laurels: "Wheaton and especially Calvin have been seedbeds of an intellectual renaissance within American evangelicalism...that has gone far beyond theology to establish a visible evangelical presence in literary scholarship, psychology, history, philosophy, and other fields." He then continues with a lengthy accolade: "From Calvin College itself emerged many of the leaders of the 'evangelical' revival: Mouw, Marsden, Plantinga, Wolterstorff, and others. Through Calvin's influence, neo-Calvinism stamped its decisive impress on many of the other leaders, including Hatch and Noll." Throughout his essay, Turner ties Calvin College's influence to its Kuyperian tradition.[9]

The October, 2000, issue of *Atlantic Monthly* contains further recognition of Calvin College. In an in-depth essay Alan Wolfe (a Jewish scholar) examines evangelical scholarship, focusing especially on Wheaton College and Fuller Seminary, but also with due attention to Calvin College. Wolfe acknowledges the influence of Abraham Kuyper and singles out early scholars such as Harry Jellema and Clarence Bouma, as well as George Marsden, Richard Mouw, Alvin Plantinga, Lewis Smedes, and Nicholas Wolterstorff. (Wolfe notes that all these worthies have left Calvin, and the current Calvin faculty was chagrined with Wolfe's unkind cut that "left

8 Hughes and Adrian, *Models*, 5,6.

9 James C. Turner, "Something to Be Reckoned With: The Evangelical Mind Awakens," *Commonweal*, January 15, 1999, 11, 13.

behind were a disproportionate number of mediocre faculty members burdened with heavy teaching loads....")[10]

In addition to the more general writings on the integration of Christianity and scholarship, Calvin scholars in many departments have also made solid contributions in "practicing" such integration in various disciplines. At the risk of neglecting to mention other deserving departments, let me single out the contributions in literature, mass communications, history, and philosophy. These departments are recognized as leaders in both Christian and secular academic circles.

(For a more extended summary of this emphasis at Calvin College and Calvin's influence in Christian higher education, see James D. Bratt and Ronald A. Wells, "Piety and Progress: A History of Calvin College," in Richard T. Hughes and William B. Adrian, *Models for Christian Higher Education*, 141-162).[11]

Denominational Affiliation

In addition to the theoretical issue of faith and scholarship, one must also ask questions about the Christian college as an institution. What does it mean to be a denominational college? Specifically, what does the relationship to a denomination mean for Calvin College? Even sketchy acquaintance with an array of Christian colleges will soon reveal the very different ways in which colleges may relate to a church. From Abilene Christian College, through countless Baptist colleges and a dozen Concordias, to Zoe College one finds a fascinating array of ownership arrangements,

[10] Alan Wolfe, "The Opening of the Evangelical Mind," *Atlantic Monthly*, October, 2000, 61.

[11] Grateful as one can be for this emphasis from the Dutch Reformed tradition, one must not assume that Calvin College had a corner on this truth. Other Christians, other Calvinists, also mined the same treasure. A fine example of this can be found in Louis H. Gunneman, *The Shaping of the United Church of Christ* (Cleveland: United Church Press, 1999). Gunneman cites "three major theological themes: the sovereign rule of God, the lordship of Christ, and the transformation of all of life" (117). He then proceeds to elaborate on these principles without so much as a glance at the Dutch Reformed tradition, but the elaboration would do Abraham Kuyper proud.

governmental structures, church requirements, and expectations of theological accountability. (Although my discussion here focuses on colleges that have a historical or legal association with a denomination, it is well to remember that other Christian colleges also have constituencies that may function like a denomination. Wheaton College, for example, has no affiliation with a particular denomination, but its constituency (supporters, alumni, and others) do exert great influence on the life of the college).

Even though it is somewhat dated, the study *Church Related Education* still is revealing in its survey of "church-relatedness." In the opening chapter,[12] by Merrimon Cuninggim, the author reviews a number of distinguishing marks of a church college that he does not find helpful. However, this catalog of misgivings does represent a very helpful list of issues and concerns that one finds in the history of Calvin College and most other denominational colleges. Here one finds, for example, the following issues: the founding of the college as a reason for control; financial support as a reason for control; board composition—clergy vs. non-clergy and church members vs. nonmembers; faculty and staff church membership; academic freedom in teaching beyond the confessional tradition; interpretation of Scripture, especially in the creation-evolution controversies; student church affiliation and/or religious commitment; required Bible and theology courses; chapel attendance; controversial speakers on campus; student behavior—from card-playing to dress codes to co-ed dorms to patriotism to interracial dating.

Cuninggim further suggests three ways in which colleges can relate to a denomination.[13] The first is the "Consonant College." Such a college is an ally to the church, generally upholding the values of the denomination but free to develop its own identity. Carleton College in Minnesota is one such school. The second model is the "Proclaiming College." The proclaiming college is a

12 "Myths of Church Relatedness," in Parsonage, *Church Related*, 17-27.
13"Categories of Church-Relatedness," in Parsonage, *Church Related*, 29-42.

witness to the church, gladly acknowledging its historical and theological ties with the parent denomination. However, the program of the college is not determined by the church; at most it is in loose partnership. Cuninggim places most religious colleges in this broad category. He does not mention Hope College (Holland, Michigan), but it probably fits here. The third is the "Embodying College," which is in many ways a reflection of the denomination. Such a college is closely tied to the history and theology of the church, and the mores and traditions are generally observed. Here one tends to find colleges in the Mennonite and Lutheran-Missouri Synod traditions. Cuninggim discusses neither the CRC nor Calvin College, but he might well have placed Calvin in this (flexible) category.

As with any taxonomy, the boundaries are fluid, the lines somewhat arbitrary, and placing a particular school in a particular category often hazardous. I will suggest, however, that Calvin College was an "embodying college" till about 1960. Up to that time it was the only CRC-related school (Dordt College began as a junior college in 1955), its faculty was (with one exception) from CRC background, as was ninety percent of its student body, and the board of trustees composed largely of CRC clergy. Even though there was dissatisfaction with the college among some constituents, Calvin was still regarded as "our school," in that it was considered to be the educational wing of the church. Scholarship, teaching, student behavior, church attendance—all of these were measured with a CRC gauge.

After 1960 many of these elements began to change, and by 1990 I would consider Calvin, in most respects, a "proclaiming college." One now finds four other colleges with strong CRC identification, thus diminishing Calvin's role as "our school." By 1990, approximately one- third of the faculty came from outside the CRC (although obliged to join), and only 64 percent of the students from CRC homes (down to 47 percent by 2000). Since 1992 the board includes non-CRC members. The support of the college among the

CRC constituency is still strong, but not as uniform as in the 1950s. Calvin's identification with the CRC also remains pronounced, but is hardly a reflection of the church. To use Cuninggim's description: As a proclaiming college, Calvin "is a free and credible witness to its being an academic partner of its proud denominational parent."

Thus a good case can be made that today (2000) Calvin operates as a proclaiming college in most respects. However, in two important ways it still is an embodying college. Calvin College is still "owned and operated" by the CRC and thus is legally still accountable to the denomination. Such accountability is seen especially in the synodical control of faculty appointments. All tenured faculty have to be approved by a synodical assembly. Secondly, all tenured faculty (with very few exceptions) have to be (or become) members of a CRC congregation or of a church in "ecclesiastical fellowship." Such a requirement is a stringent one—almost never demanded even by embodying colleges.

Calvin's relationship to the CRC can be described in many ways, but one of the most lucid descriptions is found in "An Expanded Statement of the Mission of Calvin College."[14] It is true that the description is not fully developed and somewhat idealistic and gives only a perfunctory admission to the struggles between college and church. Moreover, the other CRC-related colleges are completely ignored, even though these also function in similar ways. Still, the idea and ideal developed in this statement, that is, of "a covenantal relationship [between church and school] for mutual service in God's kingdom" is to be highly valued.

In the story that follows we will often see the stresses and pressures that accompanied the relationship, but the church and the college have been wise in maintaining the relationship. The stresses have produced changes and adjustments (synod no longer discusses the salary of individual professors!), but church and school continue

[14] This 1992 "Statement" was republished as a booklet in 1996, in tribute to provost Gordon Van Harn. See pp. 19-29, "Calvin College in Relation to the Christian Reformed Church."

to enhance each other. I am sure that the future will also bring changes and adjustments, but the covenantal relationship can endure; it is a basic and enriching element for both the denomination and the college.

2

Mother Church: A Sketch of Christian Reformed Church History

Imagine these events: Enduring Old World church persecution. Facing New World emigration. Cutting down whole forests and removing the tree stumps in order to plant a first crop of wheat. Building a log church. Sending missionaries abroad. Founding a seminary and college. Enduring heresy trials. Going through family quarrels because the children no longer want to speak Dutch. Losing a fourth of a denomination's membership.

All these events and hundreds more happened in the Christian Reformed Church. Telling 150 years of denominational history in a brief chapter is an impossibility. Fortunately, much of this history has been told elsewhere. Here I will sketch the contours of that history and highlight some of its more significant events.[1]

[1] The following titles are among the standard sources I consulted: C. Augustijn, *Abraham Kuyper: Vast en Veranderlijk* (Zoetermeer: Meinema, 1998); Henry Beets, *De Chr. Geref. Kerk in N.A.: Zestig Jaren van Strijd en Zegen* (Grand Rapids: Grand Rapids Printing, 1918); James D. Bratt, *Dutch Calvinism in Modern America: A History of a Conservative Subculture* (Grand Rapids: Eerdmans, 1984); *Classis Holland Minutes 1848-1858* (Grand Rapids: Eerdmans, 1950); Peter De Klerk, ed., *Perspectives on the Christian Reformed Church* (Grand Rapids: Baker, 1983); George Harinck and Hans Krabbendam, eds., *Breaches and Bridges: Reformed Subcultures in the Netherlands, Germany, and the United States* (Amsterdam: VU Uitgeverij, 2000); Hans Krabbendam and Larry Wagenaar, eds,. *The Dutch-American Experience: Essays in Honor of Robert P. Swierenga* (Amsterdam: VU Uitgeverij,

Dutch Background

We cannot understand the CRC in the year 2000 unless we first have a glimpse of its beginning in the 1800s. Actually, one has to begin even earlier and trace the beginnings of the Reformed, Calvinistic churches in the Netherlands to the sixteenth and seventeenth centuries. These churches were born in the cauldron of religious controversy and persecution of the Protestant Reformation, and that struggle for theological rectitude and religious freedom marked much of their subsequent history. Although beginning as a persecuted minority, the church later blossomed into a dominant, national church, with many of the attributes of a "state church."

It was also a church that underwent numerous theological controversies. Prime among these was the dispute between the strict Calvinists and the Remonstrants ("Arminians"), which culminated in the famous Synod of Dordrecht in 1618-1619 and the publication of the Canons of Dordt. Later the church suffered both from orthodox rigidity and from the spiritual virus of the Enlightenment. The reaction of the faithful believers was often to find respite in various streams of pietism.

Many of these theological and ecclesiastic forces came to serious clashes in the 1800s. Along with much of Europe, the Netherlands

2000); John Kromminga, *The Christian Reformed Church: A Study in Orthodoxy* (Grand Rapids: Baker, 1949); Henry S. Lucas, *Netherlanders in America* (Grand Rapids: Eerdmans, 1955, 1989); C. Smits, *De Afscheiding van 1834* (Oudkarspel: Nijverheid, 1971); Robert P. Swierenga and Elton J. Bruins, *Family Quarrels in the Dutch Reformed Churches in the Nineteenth Century* (Grand Rapids: Eerdmans, 1999); Robert P. Swierenga, *Faith and Family: Dutch Immigration and Settlement in the United States, 1820-1920* (New York: Holmes & Meier, 2000); Gerrit ten Zythoff, *Sources of Secession* (Grand Rapids: Eerdmans, 1987); Jacob van Hinte, *Nederlanders in Amerika* (Groningen: Noordhof, 1928); James Van Hoeven, ed., *Word and World: Reformed Theology in America* (Grand Rapids: Eerdmans, 1986); James Van Hoeven, *Piety and Patriotism* (Grand Rapids: Eerdmans, 1976); Larry Wagenaar and Robert Swierenga, eds., *The Sesquicentennial of Dutch Immigration: 150 Years of Ethnic Heritage* (Holland, MI: A.C. Van Raalte Institute, 1997); Henry Zwaanstra, *Reformed Thought and Experience in a New World* (Kampen: Kok, 1973). Also consulted: *Acts of Synod of the Christian Reformed Church; The Banner; De Wachter*, other periodical literature. The recent work by James Schaap, *Our Family Album* (Grand Rapids: CRC Publications, 1998), is a helpful popular history.

had suffered the political and spiritual tyranny of Napoleon Bonaparte, and there was much joy when the "House of Orange" was again restored to the throne. However, the new King William I proved to be more bane than blessing to the church. Along with a small coterie of state and church officials, he engineered the "Constitution [*Reglement*] of 1816," in which the church lost much of its autonomy and in some ways became a department of the government. (Its official name became *De Nederlands Hervormde Kerk NHK).* The new constitution also put a premium on theological toleration. This toleration meant, in effect, that the liberal tendencies in the church were not merely allowed but often granted preference.

Both the new governmental regulations and the liberal theology were disheartening to the more conservative, traditional wing of the church. The traditionalism came to expression especially in two ways: pietism and orthodoxy. Among both clergy and laity, one found a strong remnant of Reformed piety that fed on the books of "the Old Writers"; that hunger had more recently been nourished by an international revival (*Reveil*). Theologically there continued to be many who sought to maintain the teachings of the Reformation and of Calvinistic doctrines, coupled with a desire to establish separate Christian schools.

One important issue from the church struggle that we will meet again later in this history was the singing of hymns. The Reformed churches had largely been exclusive psalm singers. In 1807 the church had officially adopted the introduction of hymns, even though hymns were considered suspect in various parts of the church as usurpers of the psalms of David. It often was the theologically orthodox wing of the church that opposed the hymns, at least in official worship services. This opposition became fierce when the synod decided that the singing of hymns was to be obligatory. Some parishioners walked out during the singing of hymns, and a minister might protest the required hymn by covering his mouth during the singing.

Other opposition to the developments in the church took several forms. One "escape" was the conventicle—informal meetings in homes to read inspirational writings and to share in prayer and testimony. Pastors and candidates for ministry faced a more formal (and formidable) obstacle: How could they function in their ministerial office when they were at odds with the basic tenets and governance of their church?

The issue came to a head in 1834. Hendrik De Cock, a pastor in the town of Ulrum in the province of Groningen, had taken the side of those protesting the trends in the church, and he was suspended from his ministerial office. His consistory, however, supported his stance, and the congregation separated itself from the national church on October 13, 1834. This date is usually cited as the beginning of the Secession (*Afscheiding*). A number of other pastors and congregations also seceded soon after this date. Two secessionist ministers who need to be noted here particularly are Albertus Van Raalte and H.P. Scholte, who later became prominent leaders of the emigration to America.

Neither the government nor the *Hervormde Kerk* took kindly to such rebellious acts, and the secessionist pastors and their followers were harassed with fines, occasional imprisonment, the breaking up of church meetings, the billeting of soldiers in homes, and various other intimidations. Both ministers and people remained faithful to their convictions, but they also began to search for a place where they could practice a more harmonious family and church life. This search resulted in the emigration to North America.

Scholars have not always agreed on the relative importance of the secession and its aftermath in encouraging the emigration. Early historians tended to find the religious "persecution" to be the only or at least the prime motivation for the emigration of the Dutch to North America. More recent historians make a much more nuanced evaluation, and economic and social conditions (including a disastrous potato crop) in the Netherlands are also seen as major contributing factors. Nevertheless, the theological climate, the religious harassment, the church order struggles, the secularization of the schools—all of these were major factors in the move from the Netherlands.

Before we look at the emigration, however, we need to pick up another strand in the Dutch church. The 1834 Secession took place mostly in rural areas among people of pietistic bent. But there was another group in the *Hervormde Kerk* that was strongly critical of its liberal direction. And here we meet a leader whose name we will hear many times in this history: Abraham Kuyper (1837-1920).

Kuyper looms large in the history of the Dutch Reformed churches and in the history of the Christian Reformed Church. He was a minister in the *Hervormde Kerk*, became a leader of the neo-Calvinist movement, served as prime minister of the Netherlands from 1901-1905, promoted separate Christian schools and other Christian organizations, and was the founder of The Free University in Amsterdam. Kuyper was also a prodigious writer, and his influence in the Netherlands and beyond was vast. He is important in the CRC story because of his impact on the Reformed churches in the Netherlands and in North America. Kuyper led a secondary separation from the *Hervormde Kerk* in 1886 (*Doleantie*). In 1892 this separated group joined with those of the 1834 Secession to form the Reformed Churches in the Netherlands. Church historians have often characterized the two groups as follows: the people of the 1834 Secession were generally pietistic, with a strong emphasis on experiential faith; those of the *Doleantie* tended to be more intellectual and they stressed the development of a Christian culture. Both groups also strove for a return to orthodox Reformed doctrine. This characterization is simplistic, of course, but still a helpful delineation of the two emphases. In later chapters we will frequently see how these emphases keep cropping up in the history of the CRC and Calvin College.

Emigration, Settlement, and Church Strife

The story has often been told of the arrival of the Reverend Albertus Christiaan Van Raalte and some forty of his followers in western Michigan in February and March 1847 (and soon other groups in Iowa, Wisconsin, and other states). Emigration is always a daunting experience, as one faces the complete uprooting of a familiar way of life in exchange for uncertainty, new language, food, customs, and geography. If emigration in the year 2000 is difficult, how much more in the mid 1800s. One can hardly imagine the incredible obstacles as this small troop arrived by ox cart or on foot in the dense forests. Unskilled in tree felling, short of food and funds, with virtually no English, unaccustomed to the extremes of winter snow and summer heat, racked by illness and death, the vision of Van Raalte's utopian Christian community must have seemed a cruel chimera to them those first years. One marvels at their courage. They felled trees, tried to get their American gardens started, built sod huts (and later cabins and houses), learned English (usually slowly and imperfectly), organized their congregations, and founded schools.

When Van Raalte arrived in New York, he had been greeted and assisted by two pastors from the Reformed Protestant Dutch Church, Isaac Wyckoff and Thomas De Witt. This denomination (which I will usually abbreviate to "Reformed Church" or call by its current name, "The Reformed Church in America") had been founded by Dutch settlers in New York in 1628. The church remained a part of the Reformed Church in the Netherlands till 1792 and largely retained its theological traditions, but it had also been influenced by its American religious environment, such as the Great Awakening.

In 1849 this church invited the immigrants to join their fellowship, and the following year the immigrant congregations joined the Reformed Church as a separate Classis of Holland. However, the union of 1850 was soon challenged. Critics among the new immigrants charged that the Reformed Church was not sufficiently known, and that the immigrant congregations had not been consulted. Others felt that Van Raalte had assumed too much power and was forcing the churches into this union. Moreover, these critics also found practices and teaching in the Reformed Church that could not pass theological muster. Among these were theological laxity, the singing of hymns (rather than psalms), the neglect of preaching according to the Heidelberg Catechism, admitting to the Lord's Supper those who were not Reformed Christians, and the presence on the church rolls of those who were members of the Masons or other "secret societies." Van Raalte and others who remained in the Reformed Church contested these charges and found the denomination into which they had been welcomed a genuinely Reformed home.

In 1857 the issue came to a head as several ministers and congregations separated from the Classis of Holland (and the Reformed Church) to form a new fellowship. (By the end of 1857 the new church counted only one ordained minister). This separation was, of course, seen as a return to the principles of the 1834 Secession. The church called itself variously, the Dutch Reformed Church, the True Dutch Reformed Church (*Ware Hollandsche Gereformeerde Kerk*), and, after 1894, The Christian Reformed Church.

These few sentences do not begin to portray the struggle about theology, liturgical practices, ownership of church buildings, nor the clash of personalities, nor the agony of strife within families and among friends. The controversies tore apart the immigrant communities, and the relationship between the Reformed Church and the Christian Reformed Church was at times appalling. It is only within the past few decades that most of those wounds have been healed and genuine cooperation is practiced both at the congregational and the denominational level.[2]

[2] A thorough review of this history can be found in Robert P. Swierenga and Elton J. Bruins, *Family Quarrels in the Dutch Reformed Churches in the Nineteenth Century* (Grand Rapids: Eerdmans, 1999). There is no full-fledged comparative history of the two denominations, but one will find many points of comparison in James D. Bratt, *Dutch Calvinism in Modern America: A History of a Conservative Subculture* (Grand Rapids: Eerdmans, 1984).

The Christian Reformed Church, 1857-2000

In many ways the CRC developed as did other immigrant churches, such as, for example, Scandinavian Lutheran or German Mennonite churches in North America. The growth of such churches was often strongest in areas where the ethnic enclave developed, and the growth often depended directly on the number of immigrants. Another issue in all immigrant churches is a language controversy: how long does one maintain Swedish or German or Dutch in the worship services? Related to the language issue is the broader question of Americanization. The ethnic community was often insular and inward, with deliberate attempts to keep the "American" world at bay. More positively, such attempts at isolation resulted in the establishment of schools, colleges, and seminaries, as well as sanitariums, hospitals, and funeral societies.

First, the numerical growth of the denomination:[3]

	Congregations	Pastors	Families	Members
1857	4	1	130 (est)	600 (est)
1875	26	15	1,500 (est)	7,525
1887	68	40	5,069	28,240
1897	130	85	9,262	49,260
1907	167	115	12,733	66,112
1917	237	169	17,450	89,257
1927	255	201	21,681	103,920
1937	286	260	24,604	117,972
1947	315	281	31,382	134,608
1957	495	392	47,991	211,454
1967	629	544	60,282	275,530

[3] The numbers are obtained from the CRC *Yearbook*. (The first *Yearbook* was published in 1875, the second in 1881 and then annually; it was published in Dutch as *Jaarboekje* till 1918, in both Dutch and English in 1919, and in English since then). The 1857 and 1875 estimates are from *One Hundred Years in the New World* (Grand Rapids: Centennial Committee of the Christian Reformed Church, 1957), 212.

1977	706	661	66,295	288,024
1987	876	836	74,645	308,993
1997	987	Not listed	73,323	285,864

These growth figures are open to wide interpretation and analysis, but let me highlight two observations. First, the membership growth generally corresponds to high immigration figures from the Netherlands, especially from 1890-1920 and from 1947-1977. The immigration was to the United States in the early periods and primarily to Canada for the years after 1947. Secondly, the membership figures at times reflect controversies in the church. For example, the growth between 1875 and 1887 was occasioned partly by the RCA refusal to change its stand on Freemasonry (each congregation decides if the church will admit Freemasons, rather than adopting a denominational prohibition). This decision displeased the Reformed leaders in the Netherlands and they urged immigrants to join the CRC instead of the RCA. The decline between 1987 and 1997 was caused by controversies about evolution and women in ecclesiastical office—many congregations (or segments of congregations) left the CRC.

One must also note the wider geographic distribution of the denomination. In 1907 the 157 congregations were concentrated mostly in New Jersey (16), Michigan (69), Illinois (10), and Iowa (13), with the rest scattered over 11 states. By 1957 the denomination was spread over 26 states and 8 Canadian provinces, but the "clumping" was similar—147 congregations in Michigan, 30 in Illinois, and 48 in Iowa; further west, California now accounted for 22 churches. (New Jersey had increased to only 23). In Canada, of the 137 churches, 72 were located in Ontario. The ratio of congregations in various states did not change dramatically between 1957 and 1977, although overall numbers have grown considerably. The concentration in Michigan, Illinois, Iowa, and Ontario is actually larger than suggested by these numbers, since most of the larger congregations are in these regions.

Even though most of the growth of the CRC came from immigrants from the Netherlands (and from families with a dozen or more children!), the church also expanded by its mission work, both in North America and abroad. The most sustained "home missions" effort has been the work among the Navajo and Zuni Indians. Begun in the 1890s, the evangelization among Native Americans has continued till today, and the Rehoboth campus near Gallup, New Mexico, is a lasting tribute to the faithful work of many men and women. Both urban and suburban church planting has also spread the church outside of its early enclaves. Evangelization among African American, Hispanic, Korean, and other minorities has also helped to make the CRC more colorful and to broaden the church beyond its Dutch immigrant tradition.

One can probably fault the church for waiting sixty years to send its first missionaries abroad. In 1920 the first missionary families went to China, did laudable work, but soon saw their efforts devastated by terrorism and war. The missions effort in Nigeria was more sustained and was richly rewarded. The first missionary from the CRC, Johanna Veenstra, went to Nigeria under the auspices of the Sudan United Mission in 1920 but was largely supported by CRC members. Veenstra's request to have the CRC assume the mission work in Sudan was stonewalled by successive synods; finally, in 1940, the CRC took over the mission—seven years after her death. Since then the foreign mission effort has expanded to other continents, and by the end of the century the CRC had missionaries in twenty-five countries.

Two related "outreach" programs also deserve mention. In 1939 the *Back to God Hour* began as a radio broadcast on one station and has since blossomed into a world-wide radio and television ministry in nine languages. The Christian Reformed World Relief Committee, begun in 1962, has done enormously important work in hunger relief, disaster assistance, and various kinds of community development. That committee has often combined its efforts with the work of World Missions to offer exemplary word-and-deed ministry.

Among the educational ministry of the CRC one must, of course, count Calvin College and Calvin Theological Seminary. The story of Calvin College will be told in detail in this book. The origin of the seminary in 1876 is very closely related to that of the college. During the initial years, the education was intended solely for future ministers, but since their preparatory schooling was very slim, the students also needed to be instructed in nontheological subjects, often at the high school level. For a number of years the three levels—high school, college, and seminary—were taught by the same instructors, offering a dizzying array of subjects, from geography and Dutch literature to church history and isagogics. As nonministerial students were admitted, the curriculum became more diversified, and the non-theological courses eventually organized into a full-fledged college curriculum. Calvin Theological Seminary continued its education of future ministers, and today it is a respected institution offering several masters degrees and a Ph.D. program, with an enrollment of 270 students, among whom are many from other countries.

Although Calvin College is the only "official" college of the denomination, four regional colleges (see chapter 4) are also largely supported by CRC members, as is the Reformed Bible College in Grand Rapids. In addition, most CRC communities also support Christian elementary and high schools. Another denominational education venture is CRC Publications. Begun modestly in 1916 as the Publication Committee it served largely to publish the weekly magazines *De Wachter* and *The Banner*, as well as "reading sermons," and to supply Sunday school materials for students and teachers. (One of the first decisions of the new committee was to refuse announcement of gifts made to pastors). CRC Publications has grown to a significant publishing house; its most recent catalog lists some 400 titles for all areas of church life, including worship.

Most of the CRC development discussed so far has focused on growth at the denominational level. Important as all these ventures no doubt were, the real church life took place at the congregational level. What was church life like in a typical CRC congregation? Twice-a-Sunday worship services were observed dutifully—with "oncers" open to censure. Sermons were generally considered the most important feature of worship, with the length of the sermon varying from one hour (typical in 1900) to twenty-five minutes (in 2000). The CRC began as an exclusively psalm singing denomination, and choirs were taboo. Choirs became (somewhat) acceptable by 1926, and hymns were officially accepted with the 1936 *Psalter Hymnal.* As in many Protestant churches, the Lord's Supper was served quarterly (by 1990 the denominational spectrum was from weekly to quarterly), in a solemn observance. Until 1920 the standard mode of Communion included the seating of the confessing members around the Communion table, where they were served pieces of bread from a plate and wine from a common cup. Again, by 1990 there were many variations in the mode of Communion, but the most common was the serving of bread from a plate and grape juice in small individual cups, with the communicants sitting in the pews. Baptism was always uniform—the sprinkling of infants (and occasionally of adult converts). When a young person had reached "the age of discretion," she was expected to "make profession of faith"—a ceremony that included an examination by the church elders about catechism knowledge and about Christian conduct (after 1928 this examination often included the question if the confessant ever attended "the shows"), followed by a public profession during the worship service. Congregational life also included "catechism class" (a study of the Heidelberg Catechism by the church's children and youth—with teaching ranging from inspired to dreadful), and various "societies" in which the members of the church studied Scripture. Ruling and directing all of the congregation's life was the consistory, a body of elders and deacons making both frivolous and significant decisions—usually in a cloud of tobacco smoke.

Denominational Discord

The previous sketch of the history and development of the CRC generally shows a healthy growth from small immigrant beginnings to a flourishing denomination with a great degree of cohesiveness. In many ways that is an accurate picture. The CRC has been richly blessed and in various ways has been a blessing to its communities, the wider church, and many parts of the world. But that picture of growth and serenity tells only part of the story. As in all of Christendom, from the dissensions in the New Testament church of Corinth to the latest quarrel among Episcopalians, the CRC has also had more than its share of disagreements. Again, a full narrative and analysis of such disagreements is not possible here, but let me touch on a few of the controversies.

One of the most contentious disputes was "the Janssen case." Ralph Janssen was a professor of Old Testament at Calvin Seminary. He had studied in Germany (which conservatives in the church often considered a dangerous place to study theology), and soon his views became suspect. In 1919, four of Janssen's seminary colleagues brought charges of heresy against him to the Curatorium (trustees). Janssen held that some miracles recounted in Scripture might have had natural causes, he tended to stress the human rather than the divine origin of Scripture, and he was often sympathetic to the methods of "higher criticism." When the Curatorium refused to censure Janssen, the charges were laid before the 1920 synod. Again synod did not sustain the opponents. However, by 1922 the controversy had blossomed into a full-blown heresy trial, and the main item on synod's agenda was the "Janssen case." In 1921 the Curatorium had appointed an Investigatory Committee; the majority of this committee prepared a report of 152 pages in which they pilloried Janssen. In addition, a dozen communications to synod were mostly critical of Janssen's views. Since Janssen refused to appear before the synod or to submit his lecture notes, both the Investigatory Committee and the synodical examiners scrutinized students' notes of the lectures for heretical pronouncements. (Requests for copies in *De Wachter* and *The Banner* had brought these notes to light). This time Janssen did not escape the ideological noose. A twenty-two-page indictment addressed to the "Reverend and Esteemed Brethren" concludes: "With regard to *the question as to what to do with Prof. Janssen:*

Concerning this question the committee decided to submit the following as its advice to synod:

> 1) Whereas it has become evident that the instruction of Prof. Janssen, as reflected in the 'Student and Individual Notes' is unreformed in character, and
>
> 2) Whereas, prof. Janssen, through insubordination on his part has made it impossible for Synod in its investigation to go back of the 'Student Notes',
>
> Your Committee judges that Synod is called to the sad task of deposing Prof. Janssen from his office.
>
> Synod spoke its mind clearly; the report concludes with synod's vote: "*Approved in toto.*" [4]

The synod 1922 was a minor skirmish compared to the battle of 1924. Ironically, Janssen's principal opponent now came under synod's scrutiny for theological error. The Reverend Herman Hoeksema looms large in CRC history of the 1920s. Hoeksema had already raised theological eyebrows when, as a student preacher, he had prayed, "Lord, impress on the minds of the people here that when they send their children to the Public School, they send them to the portals of hell."[5] In 1920 he became pastor of the large and

4 Christian Reformed Church, *Acts of Synod,* 1922, 278. (Further references to the *Acts of Synod* will be cited in the text, with year and page number).

5 Calvin College and Seminary, Curatorium Minutes, June 1914, 9. [Further references to the Minutes of the Curatorium and of the Board of Trustees (BOT) will be indicated in the text. The minutes are housed in the Archives of the Calvin Heritage Hall collection].

prestigious Eastern Avenue congregation in Grand Rapids (where Janssen was a member) and became a leading theological light in the denomination. Hoeksema combatted Janssen in the pages of *The Banner*, was one of the four who censured him in the report of the Investigating Committee, and one of four pastors who wrote *Waar Het in de Zaak Janssen Om Gaat (What Is at Issue in the Janssen Case?)*. During one of the synod discussions about Janssen, Hoeksema rose in righteous indignation, quoting Psalm 139, "Do I not hate them, O Lord, that hate Thee? I hate them with a perfect hatred: They are become as my enemies" (*Acts of Synod*, 1922,156).

But now the prosecutor became the defendant. In several of his writings, Hoeksema (with the Reverend H. Danhof) had denied the Reformed teaching of common grace. At the 1924 synod, the writings of Hoeksema and Danhof were found wanting, and they were instructed to abide by synod's interpretation and decision about common grace. The ink was barely dry when Danhof (a delegate) informed synod while it was still in session that he would "not only protest formally against these synodical decisions, but also hope to take practical measures against them" (*Acts of Synod*, 199), and by October 1924, Hoeksema and others had launched the magazine *The Standard Bearer* which became the main vehicle to combat common grace. In 1925, Hoeksema, Danhof, and others met to form the Protesting Christian Reformed Churches, renamed in 1926 as the Protestant Reformed Churches, which took a substantial number of members from the CRC.

Other theological quarrels followed later. In the mid-sixties the Reverend Harold Dekker, professor of missions at Calvin Seminary, roiled the theological waters with several articles on limited atonement. Moreover, disagreements on the inspiration and/or authority of Scripture always simmered under the surface and frequently erupted. The dispute on creation and evolution was a major dispute in the late 1980s (see chapter 7), and the conflict about women serving in ecclesiatical office lasted from 1973-2000.

Other, less strictly theological, questions also confronted the denomination. These included women's suffrage, divorce and remarriage, the joining of labor unions, and protracted disagreement about "worldly amusements," notably movies, dance, and cards (see chapter 6). And, lest we forget—there was considerable discord about changing from the common cup to individual cup(let)s at the Lord's Supper.

These and other controversies deserve more discussion than I can offer here. Enough has been presented to show that the CRC took its doctrinal and moral teachings very seriously. The advantage of such seriousness is that orthodox doctrine and virtuous living are valued and promoted. The disadvantages are the tendency to confuse cultural mores (such as forbidding card playing) with biblical principles and the temptation to characterize one's theological opponents as heretics.[6]

As we shall see in the following chapters, these strengths and weaknesses of the CRC often come to the fore in the history of Calvin College.

[6] Again, the differences between the CRC and the RCA can be noted here. The RCA tended to be much more flexible about doctrinal differences. One can gain a quick glimpse at the different theological climates in two recent biographical sketches: James D. Bratt, "Lammert J. Hulst: The Pastor as Leader in an Immigrant Community," and Earl Wm. Kennedy, "The Summer of Dominie Winter's Discontent: The Americanization of a Dutch Reformed Seceder"; both in Krabbendam and Wagenaar, *The Dutch-American Experience*, 209-21 and 223-41.

3

Calvin College: A Very Brief History

Although much has been written about Calvin College, there is no complete history of the school. Henry Ryskamp's *Offering Hearts, Shaping Lives*[1] tells the story only to 1966, and John Timmerman's *Promises to Keep*[2] updates the history to 1974. Both of these books are extremely valuable in understanding Calvin College, especially in appreciating the people who taught and studied there.[3] A full-fledged institutional history, however, still needs to be written, and one can only hope that such a venture will be forthcoming before Calvin College's sesquicentennial or bicentennial!

In this chapter I will provide an outline of the college's history, introducing some of the more important people, events, and dates. Such an account (brief though it will be) will help provide the setting for the main theme—the relation between Calvin College and the Christian Reformed Church.

1 Henry J. Ryskamp, *Offering Hearts, Shaping Lives: A History of Calvin College 1876-1966*, ed. Harry Boonstra (Grand Rapids: Calvin Alumni Association, 2000).

2 John J. Timmerman, *Promises to Keep: A Centennial History of Calvin College* (Grand Rapids: Eerdmans, 1976).

3 Another very helpful source is George Stob, "The Christian Reformed Church and Her Schools," Th.D. dissertation, Princeton Theological Seminary, 1955.

Beginnings, 1876-1914

The preceding sketch of the beginning of the CRC can also serve as background for the origin of Calvin College. The situation in the Netherlands and in the Dutch Reformed Church, the secessions of 1834 and 1886, the emigration beginning in the 1840s, the joining and then separating from the Reformed Church in America in 1857—all these events come together in the inception of Calvin.

Initially, the only reason for offering education beyond the elementary or secondary level in the CRC community was the preparation of ministers. The new denomination needed pastors desperately, and in 1863 the Reverend W. H. Van Leeuwen and later the Reverend Douwe Vander Werp were prevailed upon to begin training young men (in their homes). In 1875 this duty was passed on to the Reverend G.E. Boer. He was inaugurated on March 15, 1876, and bravely began to teach his six students in all subjects. (This date is usually considered the beginning of Calvin College and Seminary; the date is celebrated annually at Calvin Theological Seminary in a *Dies Natalis* commemoration). "All subjects" involved not only areas usually associated with theological training, but also "preseminary" subjects, since many of the students had no college-level education or even high-school training. Dutch language and history, geography, psychology, logic, as well as Latin, Greek, and Hebrew—all these subjects were included in the curriculum. The year 1894 was pivotal, since the school was officially divided into a Literary Department and a Theological Department, and students other than aspiring ministers began to be admitted. (For some years the terminology was fluid, and the nontheological studies were also designated as academy or preparatory school.) Women students were first admitted in 1902. In 1904 the synod approved the establishment of a junior college, which was named John Calvin Junior College in 1906. In 1908, the name was changed to Calvin College, and the school continued to increase its course offerings. By September 1920, a full four-year program was in place and the first regular graduates received their B.A. degrees in 1921, although the first degree had been awarded in 1913 to Henry Meeter (later professor of Bible at Calvin), who had taken college courses elsewhere. (In chapter 4 I will discuss in detail the government of the school and its relationship to the CRC.)

This broadening of the curriculum greatly affected the growth of the school. The Theological School had started with seven students in 1876, which had increased to forty by 1890. After 1900 the growth continued as follows:[4]

	Preparatory	College	Theological	Total
1900-1901	55		17	72
1904-1905	131		16	147
1910-1911	61	33	31	125
1913-1914	220	67	26	313
1917-1918	268	64	34	336
1918-1919	283	80	42	366

Such increases in the student population obviously presented space problems. (Students apparently also wondered about the faculty's reaction to growth during a chapel service: "Principal A.J. Rooks read from the Psalms, 'O Lord, how they multiplied who rise against me'")[5] The Theological School had begun its program on the second floor of the William Street Christian School (the janitor's family occupied part of the floor). This space soon proved inadequate. In 1890, land was purchased at the corner of Franklin and Madison, and the Board of Trustees projected a new building of $25,000—a colossal sum for a small immigrant community. The solution was the first "financial drive" in Calvin's history, as the the Reverend Jacob Noordewier visited all CRC congregations to solicit funds. The building was completed in 1892 and seemed spacious and

[4] Ryskamp, *Offering Hearts*, 38.

[5] J. B. Schooland, *Living and Striving: the Emerging Pattern of My Life* (Chino, CA: Christian Printing Service, 1999), 65.

magnificent, including an auditorium for two hundred people. It was expected to serve the school for many decades, but by 1910 the board deemed it necessary to purchase property for a new campus near the outskirts of the city at Franklin and Giddings. The first building there was completed in 1917.

Housing for students presented serious problems as well. As early as 1903, two houses were used for student lodging, and in 1908, a two-story brick building on the corner of Eastern Avenue and Dunham Street was converted to dormitory space. Ryskamp sums up the living conditions there: "For a few life in the dormitory was hilarious; on the other hand, for others it was almost unbearable."[6] A more spacious dormitory was built on the new campus in 1924.

The college attempted zealously to control student conduct. An early booklet, "College Conduct" (n.d.), quoted copiously from a book of etiquette: "It is not permissible to draw up a spoonful of soup or coffee and blow upon it; one must wait until it is sufficiently cool." "A well-bred college girl . . . completes her toilette in her own room, and refrains from powdering, manicuring, or hair-dressing in public." Other precepts were adapted to the college: "The Calvinist Christian always asks the question, 'Do I, in my manner of dress, properly reflect my Christianity?'"

As the college grew, so did various student activities. The student newspaper, *Calvin Chimes,* first appeared in 1907 and has continued its (mostly illustrious) publication till today. Indeed, much of the history of Calvin can be gleaned from the pages of the *Chimes.* The college orchestra was born in 1904, various quartets and other musical groups frequently sang in area churches, and in 1923 a fledgling drama group sought to "place before students and the public dramatic productions of a high moral character."[7] Athletics were at first looked upon as a necessary evil, and basketball games with "outside groups" were frowned on by the faculty.

6 Ryskamp, *Offering Hearts,* 49.
7 Ryskamp, *Offering Hearts,* 92.

With an increase in the number of students came an increase in the size of the faculty, but one does marvel at the small number of professors and the wide array of courses they had to teach. In 1900 the Literary Department counted four teachers, and by 1919 the number of full time professors at the college had increased to only eleven; this small number meant that each professor taught various disciplines. For example, in 1900 B.K. Kuiper taught history, German, and natural science; in the 1919-1920 school year J. Van Haitsema was scheduled to teach zoology, botany, and embryology in the college, as well as geography, general science, physiology, agriculture, and geography in the preparatory school. But the professors persevered, often with long tenure. A.J. Rooks taught at the college from 1894-1941, and Henry Ryskamp served as professor of sociology and as academic dean from 1918 to 1964.

Why Calvin College?

There were, of course, various reasons for providing college education for CRC youth who were not preparing for the ministry. The first non-ministerial applicants for whom an education was deemed necessary were potential "schoolmasters." In addition, the church argued, other young people should also have opportunity for more education—but education that was safe: "We need a school for our young people, a school to which we can confidently entrust our sons and daughters, so that they will not be drenched in the poison of all kinds of errors."[8] Thus the desire grew to have young people receive an advanced education for their spiritual growth, in a protected environment, by Reformed teachers (no doubt very similar to the motivation for starting Christian colleges in other denominations). Once the college had been founded, it sought to promote the students' piety in various ways. Under "Religious Culture" in the catalog the students were reminded that the daily chapel service met at 8:00 a.m., that "on the Sabbath

[8] J. Schepers, "Een College," *De Wachter*, March 4, 1896, 2.

students are expected to worship regularly with the churches in the city," and that each student was to be visited at least once a year by a professor, "especially to be a help to the student in his religious life."[9]

There was another important reason for the promotion of a four-year college. B.K. Kuiper, an early and ardent champion for Calvin College, wrote a comprehensive rationale for a college education. His vision deserves to be quoted at some length:

> We can now finally also see our calling a little more completely. Not only as citizens of the States, but also as members of the Church, it is our calling to participate in all the activities of national life . . . . As members of the Christian Reformed Church we find our bulwark in our Reformed Confession, in the principles of Calvinism. We are to show ourselves everywhere as Calvinistic Americans....
>
> Everybody will now see clearly how the life of the church, the state, and society demand learning higher than can be taught in either the grammar or the High School, so that we cannot do without the College. But if this higher learning is necessary then we need the College also for its own sake. Then the College must train the men who later are to become teachers in the College. Then we need the College, with its libraries, museums and laboratories, as the conservatory of learning. We need the College as an intellectual center. The College is needed in order that the opportunity be provided for men to devote their whole lives, without worry, to the cause of learning, the advancement of science.[10]

[9] *Calvin College Year Book*, 1909-1910, 44.

[10] B.K. Kuiper, *The Proposed Calvinistic College at Grand Rapids* (Grand Rapids: Sevensma, 1903), 40, 50.

This aspiration was a noble vision for "the liberal arts"—although one wonders if the farmer in *De Kolonie*, toiling to clear his field of tree stumps, could muster much enthusiasm for a vision of museums and intellectual centers.

This vision of a Calvinistic education, encompassing all of life, soon found its way into the college catalog:

> Character of the College—The institution is supported mostly by the members of the Christian Reformed Church, and is controlled by the Board of Trustees of the Theological School of said church. According to the constitution all instruction given must be in harmony with "Reformed Principles." The various branches of study, therefore, are considered from the standpoint of faith and in the light of Calvinism as a life and world view. Herein lies the distinctive character of our college.[11]

Later, this rationale was expanded:

> According to the constitution all instruction given must be in harmony with Reformed principles. The various branches of study, therefore, are considered from the standpoint of faith and in the light of Calvinism as a life and world view. The aim of the college is to give young people an education that is Christian, not merely in the sense that devotional exercises are appended to the ordinary work of a college but in the larger and deeper sense that all the class work, all the student's intellectual, emotional and imaginative activities shall be permeated with the spirit and teaching of Christianity.[12]

One of the more expansive treatments of this theme appeared at the semicentennial celebration. Louis Berkhof, long-time professor and president at the seminary, set forth in some detail "Our

11 *Calvin College Year Book 1911-12, 34.*
12 *Calvin College Year Book* 1917-18, 36.

School's Reason for Existence and the Preservation Thereof." Borrowing from John Calvin and especially Abraham Kuyper, he propounded what has often been repeated since:

> There is still another consideration. Calvinism is not merely a system of doctrine—in fact, in that sense the name may be considered a misnomer; it is also a view of the world and of life in general. It is only through the instrumentality of high class agencies of education that a comprehensive system like Calvinism can be expounded and developed and propagated and exhibited in all its bearings on practical life. Moreover, it calls for schools that honor the Word of God as a light also on the pathway of science, and that make the principles of the Reformed faith fundamental in all their teachings; schools in which religion is the leaven that leaveneth the whole lump.
>
> Our College is dedicated to that great purpose. It finds its reason for existence in the Reformed principles for which we stand. The great task to which it is expected to address itself, is to apply these principles in every field of study, as the nature of the case may demand, and to exhibit their bearing on life in all its phases. [13]

As we will see later, this emphasis on a Calvinistic world-and-life view (an awkward translation of the Dutch *wereldbeschouwing*) appears again and again in the history of Calvin College.

Ryskamp, in *Offering Hearts,* discusses in considerable detail the emerging curriculum and the difficult choices that had to be made about adding courses and programs (see especially chapter 8). Certainly the vision of B.K. Kuiper and Louis Berkhof was an underlying principle that guided the decisions. But another factor was at work as well—university prerequisites and the accreditation of each program by the University of Michigan. As students applied

13 *Semi-Centennial Volume, Theological School and Calvin College 1876-1926* (Grand Rapids: Theological School and Calvin College, 1926),130-31.

for further study (for example, at the University of Michigan and the University of Chicago), they often discovered lacunae in their Calvin education, and they urged the college to prepare its students more adequately. Thus, in addition to seeking to provide a nurturing spiritual environment and a Reformed, Calvinistic perspective, there also was the reality of American academic life that shaped the college and its curriculum.[14]

Transitional Years, 1914-1920

It is of course always difficult to pinpoint the beginning and end of periods and eras within a history. So it is with the history of Calvin College. But we can reasonably consider 1876-1914 as years of beginning, 1914-1920 as transitional years, and 1920-1945 as the next era.

Even though the United States did not enter World War I until the spring of 1917, the Great War did greatly affect American life. For the Dutch immigrant community, the impact of the war diminished their (self-imposed) isolation from American national life and hastened the Americanization process. Language was one important aspect of this process. Since the war produced violent anti-German emotion in America, the Dutch (and the Dutch language) were often confused with Germany, and the use of Dutch forcibly curtailed.[15]

[14] Calvin's closest collegiate neighbor and sister school faced the same dilemma. In his inaugural address, President Wynand Wichers of Hope College in Holland said, "The college must remain loyal to the denomination which gave it birth and it must at the same time cater constantly to the accrediting agencies which set the scholastic standards" (*Hope College Anchor*, October 14, 1931, 5).

[15] The Curatorium Minutes of 1918 provide interesting documentation on this issue. The Curatorium discussed the allegations in the *Michigan Tradesmen* that Calvin was "a hotbed of pro-German ideas and prejudices and propaganda, and that some of the professors are doing their utmost to plant the seeds of sedition and treason" (27). Also of concern were those professors who did not speak adequate English to be able to lecture in that language. Moreover, "the Curatorium has weighed the issue if in the theological subjects there is enough awareness of American life—the place where in God's providence we have been placed" (19). Of course, the minutes (and presumably the discussion) were all in Dutch!

These years can also be characterized as ones of internal transition. At Calvin College, writes Ryskamp, "Between 1914 and 1920 the faculty was engaged in almost continuous discussion of college programs,"[16] and by the end of that time the curriculum had become solidified, with the fourth year finally in place by 1920. Also, the various preprofessional programs became established at this time. As important, the college appointed its first president in 1919. Up to this time the administration had been largely in the hands of the faculty (with the curatorium at times second-guessing the faculty). The appointment of the Reverend J.J. Hiemenga as president (no consideration was given to any non-clergy candidate) marked another step into becoming an "American college." Finally, the building and occupation of the new campus and of the main building (with three science laboratories) at Franklin and Giddings in 1917 further indicated the transition to a new era.

Years of Struggle, 1920-1945

The life of Calvin College during these decades must be seen in the context of American life and culture. All I can do here is merely to allude to the social and moral upheavals of the 1920s, the Great Depression of the 1930s, and World War II from 1939-1945. Moreover, the denominational life of the CRC experienced some of its most stressful times in the 1920s. Certainly the lives of faculty and students were greatly affected and conditioned by these events.

During this period the first five presidents of the college also made their mark. A brief paragraph about each will have to suffice.

President *J.J. Hiemenga* (1919-1925) was chosen because he was a well-known minister, a fine preacher, and an engaging leader, who had a good track record of overseeing building projects in the congregations he had served. One of his achievements was the elimination of the preparatory school which was turned into Grand Rapids Christian High School. He was also the first to give shape

16 Ryskamp, *Offering Hearts*, 61.

to the office of the president. This shaping did not come without considerable struggle. The faculty had been accustomed to directing most affairs of the college and they grudgingly gave up some of their authority. Hiemenga also undertook the task of all American college presidents—raising funds; he successfully garnered the funds for the building of the dormitory/gymnasium, built in 1924.

When Hiemenga returned to pastoral work, the board of trustees appointed *Johannes Broene*, professor of psychology, as acting president for one year. But he remained in the position from 1925-1930. Ryskamp speaks highly of Broene's presidency. The faculty appreciated him, because he did not further curtail their authority, and the board had confidence in him. "The administration of Broene was just what could be expected—good, highly respected by the constituency. . . a time of quiet growth."[17] Growth in the student body was due partly to the increased number of women students—an increase that necessitated the appointment in 1926 of the first "Adviser to the Girls," Johanna Timmer.

R.B. Kuiper, the next president (1930-1933), was again a popular preacher—who soon discovered that the office of president did not really require his ministerial skills. After his resignation he wrote the board: "I have learned that the work of the president is necessarily in very large measure administrative. I question whether it is the proper work of a minister of the gospel. Surely the position does not require a minister" (BOT Minutes, 1933, #108). Of course, the next two presidents were ordained clergymen! During Kuiper's administration, the North Central Association of Secondary Schools and Colleges gave its first formal approval to Calvin College and its programs. Also during this time, the Calvin Thespians was organized, "to produce at least one play a year for public entertainment, a play worthy of presentation in our circles."[18]

President Kuiper, further, had the unenviable opportunity to oversee the reduction of faculty salaries—and even those reduced

17 Ibid, 84.
18 *Calvin College Prism* 1933, 54.

salaries were at times in arrears. The appalling economic conditions can be gauged by a few sentences from Kuiper's financial report: "To be sure, we are two months in arrears in the payment of salaries, but that is due to the fact that the Grand Rapids Savings Bank has not been reopened since the banking holiday. Our impounded account is equal to what is owing on salaries. When, how, and whether this account will be released is very uncertain" (BOT Minutes, 1933, # 44).

During Kuiper's tenure there also were a number of serious problems simmering. These problems tended to cluster around the question of whether Calvin College was clearly and constantly a Calvinistic, a (Christian) Reformed college. Student behavior was questioned because of some of the student writing in *Chimes* and especially because of student movie attendance. The teaching of some professors was suspect, and there was concern about the increasing number of non-CRC students.

Some of these issues came to a head during the presidency of *Ralph Stob* (1933-1939). Stob had been a popular professor of Greek at the college, but proved to be less congenial as a president. He took seriously the mandate of the board to guarantee that the college be thoroughly Reformed in both teaching and life-style. The life-style issue that proved most contentious was student attendance at movies and the predicament of the administration and faculty called upon to monitor such attendance. President Stob assumed an aggressive posture in dealing with this and other student infractions and found the students less than enthusiastic about his policies. The main discord with the faculty was the teaching of Harry Jellema of the philosophy department. Stob had been censorious of Jellema when they were colleagues, and now that he was president, he pressured Jellema more severely; Jellema resigned and took a position at the University of Indiana. (He rejoined Calvin from 1947-1963 and became one of Calvin's most influential teachers). The board received complaints about the president but decided to reappoint him: "The present unrest in faculty and student body in regard to the present administration can be settled, if the Board of Trustees stands firmly behind the president" (BOT Minutes 1935, #122). However, by 1939 the unrest had achieved such momentum that Stob was not reappointed.

The following year was a bizarre year administratively. Professor Johannes Broene was again asked to serve as acting president for one year. He acquiesced reluctantly, but his was a caretaker administration. More power was wielded by a committee appointed by synod to investigate both students and faculty at the college. This Committee of Ten acted with great ardor and tried to remake the college in short order. Neither students nor faculty appreciated the attempt. Under the headline, "Our Right to be Heard," the editor of *Chimes* expostulated: "We are making here the plea that we students be no longer regarded as a group of infants who must have their problems solved for them...."[19] The main item of contention was, again, the question of movie attendance. The faculty chafed under the suspicion and the peremptory methods of the committee, especially when the committee took it upon itself to recommend the name of the next president.

This contentious period came to an end with the appointment of the Reverend *Henry Schultze* as president (1939-1951). Schultze was a professor at the seminary and a respected voice in the denomination; his presidency was in many ways a harmonious one. Of course, it was also a difficult time, as he steered the college through the war and post-war years.

The war made a deep impact on the college, as it did on all of American life. The most noticeable impact was the drop in male students; women student actually moved into the men's dormitory, while the men moved to smaller quarters. The total enrollment in 1941 was 520, and by 1944 it had declined to 420. Schultze's greatest test came two years later when the enrollment rose to 1,245.

In summarizing the years 1920-1945, I have focused mostly on the administrative aspects of the college. Of course, student life

[19] November 15, 1939, p. 5.

went its way—often unaware of or uninterested in the issues that concerned presidents and professors. A catalog of events that especially concerned students would include the following:

The *Prism* was first published in 1920 and dutifully chronicled the diverse clubs and organizations, from the Blotter to the Phytozoon Clubs. Debates and orations flourished in the 1930s. Peter De Vries, Frederick Manfred, Meindert and David C. De Jong (all of whom later became nationally known authors) sharpened their writing talents at the college. Students welcomed the (first) Hekman Library in 1928, and they often chafed under compulsory chapel attendance. The Girls Glee Club was founded in 1925, and women students started moving into "coops" (cooperative houses) in 1940. Preseminary students struggled through their nineteen hours of Dutch (plus a required course in Dutch history), twenty hours of Greek, fourteen hours of Latin, and eight hours of German. The introduction of summer sessions during World War II helped students who had deferred military service complete their studies in three years. The growth of athletics and competitive sports was also welcomed. Men's basketball did not have an auspicious start: in 1920 the team lost its first game against Hope College 30-13. The rivalry between the two schools was fierce: "One of the first games with Hope was followed by such a destructive aftermath—defacing property, raucous verbal exchange, and the crunch of fists—that competition was temporarily abandoned."[20] And, of course, garnering tuition was a constant challenge. Here geography made a difference: "For students residing west of the Mississippi River but east of Montana, Wyoming, Colorado, and New Mexico, the tuition is thirty-three and one-half dollars per semester; for two students from one family residing in the region defined, the tuition for each is twenty-seven dollars a semester."[21] From the perspective of 2001, the amount looks ridiculously low, but to families of the

[20] Timmerman, *Promises,* 65.
[21] *Calvin College Year Book*, 1934-1935, 15.

Depression, many of whom had just lost their farms, the twenty-seven dollars was often beyond reach.

Years of Growth and Growing Pains, 1945-2000

The years from 1945 to the present are even more filled with events and names than the Calvin College years before that; we therefore have to be even more selective in highlighting important issues and persons.

The chief development in the post-war years was the sudden increase in enrollment. In 1945 Calvin had 503 students; this number increased to 1,245 by 1946. A few sentences from the "Report of the College President," February 1947, will demonstrate the burden for the administration: "...shortage of faculty members, a shortage of classroom facilities, a shortage of housing." "The provision of proper eating facilities for our students was also a major problem." "The faculty of Calvin has been burdened with exceedingly heavy loads..., but there was no grumbling." "The use of the library has tripled." Various make-shift arrangements were made during the initial years of higher enrollment. The expansion of the library (1950), the new science building (1950), and the commons (1953) helped alleviate the space problem, but by 1954 the board decided to halt further building until a master plan for campus expansion could be developed. President Schultze, who was frequently ill during these years, continued to provide fine leadership and, in 1947, spearheaded the largest financial campaign up to that time: one million dollars.

William Spoelhof, who had been professor of history at Calvin since 1946, became president in September 1951 and remained in office untill 1976. Timmerman captures Spoelhof's contribution well: "He has been an uncommonly gifted president during uncommonly difficult years."[22] No doubt part of these "difficult years" was an issue Spoelhof inherited from the spring of 1951, when seven

[22] Timmerman, *Promises*, 162.

preseminary students (soon dubbed "The Sacred Seven") asserted that "man is being enthroned at Calvin College, rather than God," and accused six faculty members of various kinds of secularism.[23] In later years Spoelhof had to deal with more than his share of controversies, many accusing the faculty of an assortment of heresies (some of which will be discussed in chapter 7).

Charges of student misconduct were also rife. (See chapter 6 for details.) The (perennial) issue of students succumbing to worldly amusements continued to be a source of contention. The college administration was finally relieved of the burden of supervising students' movie attendance with a synodical decision of 1966. The "moving picture theater," the "shows," the "movies" were rebaptized as "film arts" and "legitimate cultural mediums," which could be used with discrimination. This period also included the political and social upheavals of the sixties and seventies, and although Calvin students did not engage in riots and bra-burnings, the atmosphere on campus was often tense, and the constituency found much wanting in student behavior. The most voluminous archival file of letters from Spoelhof's tenure is the one of documenting the *Bananer* episode—the student spoof issue of the denominational magazine, *The Banner*, in 1970 (discussed in chapter 6). The constituents' frustration with Calvin seemed to become crystallized by this clever but irreverent bit of journalism.

The most momentous change in the curriculum occurred in the mid-sixties. A three-year study by the curriculum study committee resulted in a comprehensive report, *Christian Liberal Arts Education* (accepted by the faculty in 1965, published in 1970 by Eerdmans). The document outlines masterfully the contours of Christian (Reformed) higher education and spells out its curricular implementation. For the students, the most noticeable difference was the 4-1-4 schedule: two semesters in which the student was to take four courses, and an interim with concentrated study in one

[23] Ryskamp discusses this episode in some detail (*Offering Hearts*, 134-36).

course. The one new course that proved most significant was Christian Perspectives on Learning (CPOL), an interdisciplinary course dealing with foundational religious issues, normally taken by students in their freshman year.

The other major achievement in Spoelhof's administration was the move to the Knollcrest campus. By 1954 it had become clear that the college could expand no further on the Franklin campus, and the board investigated various relocation plans. In 1956, the college purchased the 166-acre Knollcrest estate on the outskirts of the city—to the anguished cry of many in the constituency, about so much space and so much money. (The $9 million projected cost for the property and a future campus seemed a staggering sum). The question of regional (junior) colleges was often the background for the skepticism: "Two thirds of the students of Calvin College are in the first two years. If they would be taken out and if Michigan like western Iowa would adopt Junior Colleges we would have enough room for the next 40 years. Let us be careful about going in debt that we can't pay, for that is stealing."[24] But the college and seminary did move to Knollcrest. The seminary building was completed in 1960, the library-classroom in 1962. The college operated (inconveniently) with a split campus until 1973, and the construction of new buildings continued apace. During these years the sterling work of Henry De Witt, vice president for building and finance, earned him the well-deserved moniker, "Builder of Calvin."

Anthony Diekema, who had been associate chancellor of the University of Illinois Medical Center, assumed the presidency in Calvin's centennial year; he served from 1976-1995. The building program mentioned in the previous paragraph continued during his tenure. So did an incredible amount of fund raising. I mentioned the financial campaign of 1947, when a million dollars was raised. Diekema's administration saw a series of very successful financial campaigns. These efforts were climaxed in the "Campaign for Calvin," which at its conclusion in 1996 had reached $58.75 million.

24 Discussion at Synod 1957, reported in *The Banner*, August 9, 1957, 4.

Significant scholarly development can be seen in the institution of the Calvin Center for Christian Scholarship (1977), the Multi-Cultural Lectureship (1980), the H.H. Meeter Center for Calvin Studies (1982), and the beginning of an MA in Christian Studies. The Multi-Cultural Lectureship was an attempt to give more visibility to minority groups both in North America and worldwide. This effort was part of a comprehensive plan to have Calvin become a more ethnically diverse institution, both in student body and faculty. Included in this plan was Mosaic, a $3 million campaign for a multicultural endowment, as well as a Minority Graduate Fellowship Program. These programs bore fruit, but the percentage of minority students and faculty remained very small. Ideologically the curriculum became more self-consciously "Kuyperian," as the "faith-and-learning" emphasis drew heavily on the tradition of Abraham Kuyper.[25]

In terms of keeping the students in check, Diekema's administration was aided by a series of synodical decisions and a major report on dance, which (as the Film Arts report had in 1966) changed the terminology and rhetoric, so that now dance was to be seen as "an area of human life to be brought under the lordship of Christ" (*Acts of Synod*, 1982, 571). But there continued to be collisions between students and administration: in 1977 Diekema banned the showing of *A Clockwork Orange,* and controversies with the Film Arts Committee continued, as films such as *Taxi Driver* and *Oh, God!* were shown on campus. However, Diekema's most crucial tussle was not about student conduct, but about faculty teaching and writing, especially the controversy about creation and evolution, which included the bizarre accusation that Diekema was one of the four horsemen in the Book of Revelation (see chapter 7).

An issue far removed from student concern, but very significant for the college, was a change in governance. In 1991, Calvin College and Calvin Theological Seminary officially became separate

[25] See James D. Bratt and Ronald A. Wells, "Piety and Progress," in *Keeping Faith: Embracing the Tensions in Christian Higher Education* (Grand Rapids: Eerdmans: 1996), 40-43.

institutions with separate boards of trustees—completing a process of separation that had been in progress for several years. The next year's synod approved a change in which a college board member no longer needed to be Christian Reformed, but a "professing member in good standing of a church body within the Presbyterian and Reformed confessional tradition of Christianity" (*Acts of Synod*, 1992, 604).

Spoelhof and Diekema led the college for a combined forty-four years. The arrival in 1995 of *Gaylen Byker* as the next president was therefore a signal event. Spoelhof and Diekema were both professional academicians, whereas Byker's professional career was largely in the business sector. No doubt one factor in this selection was the awareness that American college presidents spend much of their time raising funds—and a person from the business world would be able to provide financial leadership. President Byker soon proved his financial acumen: in 1998 the college received two grants of $10 million for campus expansion—one building to be a new facility for communications and the other for a conference center. A building completed in 1999 was the John ("Doc") De Vries Hall of Science, to be used especially for medical education and research.

Several new programs were also begun. In 1998, the Paul B. Henry Institute and Chair in Christianity and Politics was founded, as was the Institute for Christian Worship (cosponsored by Calvin Seminary). Pathways to Possibilities, a community outreach program (initially funded by the Kellogg Foundation) allowed Calvin to partner with Grand Rapids inner city churches, with the special aim of keeping youths in school. Two other programs that have flourished in recent years are the January Series of prominent lecturers and the Festival of Faith and Writing.

Of course, not all of campus life is reflected in the annual "President's Report" or the alumni magazine, *Calvin Spark*. The student paper, *Chimes,* made sure that other events were reported as well. A headline in a 1996 issue read: "Calvin women cope with unexpected pregnancy," and, in 1997, "Suicide attempts not uncommon at Calvin." Controversial issues included extended discussions (and disagreements) on homosexuality, and the president apologized to the community in April, 1999, for the appearance (and language) of singer Liz Phair.

In these years, the main issue involving Calvin's relationship to the CRC was not so much constituency critique of the faculty as internal campus disagreement over the requirement that all Calvin faculty are to be members of the CRC and have to send their children to a Christian elementary and high school. Extended (and passionate) discussions on the faculty listserv "Calvin-Matters" demonstrated strong disagreement about the requirement.

Some students took a lively interest in all of the issues just mentioned. Others, I presume, were more exercised about the increasing prohibitions on smoking. And all students took great comfort from the *Chimes* 1999 headline: "Historic Hope Streak Broken. Calvin Beats Hope for the First Time in Five years." No one at Calvin needed to be reminded that the reference was to a basketball game.

This overview of Calvin College has often singled out presidents and their achievements (and agonies). It goes without saying that such a focus does great injustice to hundreds of staff and faculty, as well as thousands of students. Those professors and students in many ways *are* Calvin College. Let me again remind readers that Ryskamp's and Timmerman's books are wonderful windows on students and faculty. The chapters that follow will also do more justice to the total life of the college.

4

Onze School: The Ties That Bind

Although this study deals with the history of Calvin College from the "official" founding in 1876, it is well to keep in mind that there was no institution by that name until 1908. The school founded in 1876 was simply called *De Theologische School*, and the nontheological students admitted in 1894 attended the "Literary Department." In 1906, the designation "John Calvin Junior College" was first used, and after 1908, "Calvin College."

In the previous chapter we saw the motivation for the establishing of post-secondary education for all the youth of the church. The need for such education was seen both as a way to ward off the evils of Americanism and American education and of establishing the principles and practices of Calvinism. The desire for a Christian college was very strong in the denomination.

However, one finds much less unanimity on the control of and funding for such a school. As soon as the desire for a "Literary Department" was posed, there was opposition. A writer in the Dutch language church paper *De Wachter* began the discussion. Ireneus (pen name for the Reverend Henry Vander Werp) raised the question: Why should the denomination as a whole raise funds? "It seems to me unreasonable to have the whole Church pay for an Institution from which the citizens in Grand Rapids will profit the most."[1] This objection and others continued in some form for the next century. I will sketch the main arguments for and against denominational control, as well as synodical decisions on church control, in roughly chronological order.

Should the Church Own the College?

One of the earliest proponents of a church college was the Reverend Klaas Kuiper. (The reader of CRC history will have a difficult time keeping track of all the Kuipers in this story. Klaas became an early "Mr. Calvin College" before there was such a college.) He reiterated both the importance of Reformed education and the role of the church in this venture: "...why should it not be the calling of all the members of the church, of the whole church?"[2]

But two years later synod already began to question the propriety of such sponsorship. It declared flatly that the church may not run a college (*Acts*, 1900, 58). Rather, a college should be sponsored by an association (although the church might financially support such a venture). In the next three years, the church made a valiant attempt to organize such an association of paying members. Several leaders stumped the denomination, among whom was the Reverend Henry Beets (later editor of *The Banner*), who gave, according to his own report, "little talks of nearly two hours," but complained that for some of his talks he had "a rather small gathering." Valiant efforts and pumped-up oratory did not, however, produce the hoped-for association. In retrospect, Beets concluded: "The great majority of the people were not open to the idea of adopting the Dutch method of having a separate association of higher education. They preferred, consciously or subconsciously, the American way

1 "Meer Uitgebreid Lager Onderwijs," *De Wachter*, Oct 11, 1893, 1.
2 Klaas Kuiper, "Editorial," *De Wachter*, September 14, 1898, 3.

of doing things, and the School remained the School of the Churches...."[3]

The concerted effort of recruiting members and raising funds was not repeated in later years, but the vision of an association-operated school did not expire. Even though synod 1908 ruled that sponsorship did not have to be decided on principial grounds but could be decided more practically, such American practicality was heresy to the opponents of church control. Between 1900 and 1920 the issue was debated at great length and with greater heat. Two theological adversaries illustrate the positions staked out.

Klaas Kuiper continued to defend a church-sponsored and church-financed college. Although much more loquacious than in 1895, his basic argument did not change. The church is responsible for the future of its youth. This responsibility includes the education of young people. "We do not say that the church *must*, but the church *may* found a college." We can, he continues, learn from the Presbyterians. They do not endlessly debate such questions. Like good practical Americans, if they see the need for a college, the church will start one.[4] A decade later Kuiper again (still?) urged the church to enlarge its vision of education. Instead of being concerned only with the training of pastors, one must envision a school from which will come, "Christian doctors, Reformed missionaries, Reformed teachers, Reformed nurses for the ill and mentally deranged."[5]

Among opponents of church control, the Reverend F. Ten Hoor, long-time professor at the seminary, took pride of place. In four leisurely articles in *De Gereformeerde Amerikaan,* he set out his views on the relationship between the CRC and the college.[6] He criticizes previous synods at length for their ambiguous or erroneous

3 Henry Beets, *De Christelijke Gereformeerde Kerk in Noord Amerika* (Grand Rapids: Grand Rapids Printing Co., 1918), 298.

4 Klaas Kuiper, "Aan mijn Vriend iii," *De Wachter*, April 8, 1903, 2.

5 Klaas Kuiper, "Een Lang Gevoelde Behoefte,"*De Wachter*, September 16, 1914, p. 3.

6 F. M. Ten Hoor, "De College en de Kerk," *Gereformeerde Amerikaan*, 14, 1-4 (January-April, 1910).

statements. Chief among these is that the synods were ready to have practical concerns determine their posture. "Principle is just pushed aside. May we do that? If it really is a principle, then it rests in God's ordinance.... It is certainly clear enough that we may not do this."[7] However, Ten Hoor is especially censorious of the admission that an association-controlled arrangement would be "more pure," but that a church-controlled college is still considered permissible. In Ten Hoor's theology there is no space for more or less pure views. A position is either right or wrong. If association control is right, church control is wrong: "That is in principle not less pure, but it is against the principle [*beginsel*]."[8] A church is to be engaged only in ecclesiastical affairs—only those activities which are directly related to or necessary for its mission. A college, however, is not essential for the life of the church.

In his final article Ten Hoor indicates most clearly why the church may not operate a college. The college (higher education for all areas of life) belongs to our natural, temporal life, to our existence as human beings and citizens. The church, on the other hand, is in the spiritual realm, it is created by Christ for the salvation of the world. These two realms must remain separate. This is not to say that a college need not be Christian. Of course it should be. So must all of life. "A commercial association and an association for a butter factory must also be Christian in their work..., but it does not follow that they belong to the terrain of the church or must be controlled by the church. As associations they belong to civic life. It is the same with a college and also with a university."[9]

Ten Hoor's argument often took a somewhat different slant when used by authors invoking Abraham Kuyper's theory of "sphere sovereignty." Put briefly, Kuyper suggested that each area of life, such as the state or church or school, has its own purpose and structure, as well as its own authority. Thus the state may not

7 Ten Hoor, "De College," 155.
8 Ibid., 150.
9 Ibid., 213.

control the church, since the church must exercise its own "sovereignty." In the same way, the church may not control the school. When debating the government of Calvin College, the opponents of church control often hitched Kuyper to their theological wagon.

The writers of overtures and reports to synod were also busy, and the remainder of this historical sketch is told best by looking at this discussion. Between 1908 and 1934, virtually every synod was presented with a request to re-study the matter or to rescind previous decisions—that is, every overture was an attempt to eliminate (or at least decrease) the involvement and control of the church. During this time the longest study was presented in 1926 (*Agenda for Synod*, 27-42). At times synod spent many hours and pages on (re)studying the question, at other times it gave a brief "not-that-again" response.

The synods always returned to two arguments. First, even though the main task of the church is not education, it is not *wrong* for the church to be involved in education. Put differently, it may be more proper for an association to control a college (that is a *zuiver*, "pure" principle), but the church certainly has a derived obligation. The second response was a more practical one: the time is not right for a change. The favorite word was *voorloopig*—for the time being. The church should continue its current control *voorloopig*, because the financial situation demanded it. Or, the church should continue to be involved, because the people were not ready to form an association to be responsible for the school. Several synods proclaimed that the people were *niet rijp*—that is, not ripe or mature enough.

The issue did not receive much attention from 1934-1953. But then the question cropped up again—for at least two reasons. One was the emerging influence of post World War II Dutch immigrants. In the Netherlands these immigrants had continued to be captivated by Abraham Kuyper's ideas. A fundamental theory of Kuyper that now resurfaced was the notion that each social "sphere" or association should be sovereign in its own domain, that is, the church should not intrude upon an educational institution. In addition, the Dutch had experienced several generations of separate Calvinistic (as well as Roman Catholic and Socialistic) organizations, from political parties to goat breeding clubs. Thus the idea of a Calvinistic association for higher education (to control Calvin College) seemed not only principially correct, but also perfectly possible. Dutch Calvinists had always done it that way! Since most of these immigrants settled in Canada, many (but not all) of the overtures originated in Canadian congregations.

A second reason for the resurfacing of the church control issue was the establishment of several regional colleges in the CRC community. Dordt College in Sioux Center, Iowa, was begun in 1955; Trinity Christian College in Palos Heights, Illinois, in 1959; King's College in Edmonton, Alberta, in 1979; Redeemer College in Ancaster, Ontario, in 1982. The founding and success of these colleges proved that association control was possible in North America. Synod's standard response, "Our people are not ready for giving association support," was no longer a feasible excuse. Moreover, another issue resurfaced. In 1893 Ireneus had complained about sending money to Grand Rapids. Now that complaint took on new meaning: "Why should we pay for a college in Grand Rapids when we already support a college in Sioux Center and Palos Heights?"

Again, synods alternated between brush-offs and careful listening. Synod 1952 ruled that the situation "does not warrant another study," and synod 1968 harrumphed with one sentence: "The time does not seem to be auspicious." But other synods were more responsive. One of the most careful reports to appear in this long history was presented in 1957. Since the committee was a "balanced" committee, it predictably came with a majority and two minority reports. But again, synod refused to budge. It repeated that perhaps the church had no direct scriptural mandate to operate a college, but it certainly had the "derived right" to do so.[10] More overtures were presented to succeeding synods, but the delegates were no more ready to change course than the esteemed fathers and brethern of a century previous. During the 1970s and 1980s the principial argument about sphere sovereignty continued to be voiced, but the presence of several other colleges made the regional issue (with its financial implications) come to the fore with new urgency. For example, a 1988 overture for privatization (now the preferred term) from Classis Chatham listed Dordt, Trinity, The King's, and Redeemer as Christian Reformed colleges—"church related, but not denominationally owned." However, these schools are not supported in the same manner: "The quota support for it places Calvin College in a preferential position over the other CRC colleges" (*Acts*, 363). After 1988 most of the discussion centered on a more equitable distribution of denominational quotas (later: ministry shares), and by 1991 the issue was submerged in the study on the separation of the college and the seminary.

Denominational control of Calvin College was a century-long discussion. I doubt if there have been many colleges that have deliberated about their relationship to a parent body so long and so arduously with so little effect. The arguments were often presented with great passion and theological acumen, with various nuances and emphases. However, the main arguments remained the same. Those opposed to denominational control argued that the church may not operate a college, since Scripture does not grant that task to the church. Moreover, Reformed theology, especially as developed by Abraham Kuyper, teaches that a school should have its own sphere of authority. The *practical* arguments usually centered on the financial support for the college. At first the opponents argued that the required support of Calvin College by all regions favored

[10] One of the members of Minority Report 2 was George Stob. His doctoral dissertation, "The Christian Reformed Church and her Schools" (Princeton Theological Seminary,1955), is an extremely fine history of the Christian school movement and of Calvin College and Seminary. In his dissertation Stob already made a strong case against denominational control of the college.

families in the Grand Rapids area, since the youth from Paterson, New Jersey, or Luctor, Kansas, would not be able to attend. Later, with the rise of regional colleges, the regional argument shifted slightly: those who were supporting regional colleges should not be forced to support a Michigan college as well.

The responses for the status quo did not change greatly either. Although proponents of church control often acknowledged that association control might be theologically more "pure," they always insisted that the church had a secondary or derived obligation to educate its youth. So with the question of "readiness." Synod 1910 decided that it was not the appropriate time to make any changes in the church's control of the college (*Acts*, 42). Eighty years later, synod 1990 determined that this was "not the proper time to 'privatize' the college" (*Acts*, 28).

Thus the CRC continued to "own" Calvin College. From the fledging junior college in 1904, a four-year college program by 1919, through a flourishing college of over four thousand students by the end of the century, Calvin has been the denomination's school. In terms of financial support, prayers, and concern, as well as a 125-year procession of faculty, staff, and students, the CRC has demonstrated its sense of responsibility for Calvin College.

But the CRC saw no reason to separate responsibility from control. If the church provided its young people with a Reformed college education, the church could and should also see to it that the college carried out its mandate; faculty and students were watched closely to determine if they were worthy representatives of Our School. In the pages that follow we will see how this sense of responsibility (often sacrificial responsibility) and the desire for control were exercised.

Reformed Foundation

The early founders loved the expression, "*op Gereformeerde grondslag*"—on a Reformed foundation. The idea of establishing a college made sense to them only if its foundations were Christian, if its education was imbued with Reformed, Calvinistic principles. These principles included, of course, the theological teachings as embodied in the church's confessions, such as the doctrine of election, and later the interpretations on creation and evolution. In addition, the teachings of Abraham Kuyper, that all of learning and all of life was to be subject to the rule of Christ, became foundational to Calvin College. More specifically, this Kuyperian influence led to an emphasis on the integration of faith and learning. By 1952 the "Board Report" to synod mentioned "That Perennial Problem of Integration," citing both achievements and problems, as well as constituency dissatisfaction (*Acts*, 1952, Supplement 29-A) .

Op Gereformeerde grondslag also came to include non-academic issues, and soon Christian Reformed traditions and mores about worldly amusements and church attendance came under constituency scrutiny. (In chapters 6 and 7 we will examine some of the issues on which the church and the college were at odds). Always in the background is the assumption voiced early in the college's history: "Even though the College will eventually become more independent, the Church will guarantee that the education will continue to be based on Reformed principles" (*Acts*, 1904, Art. 89).

Finances

Finances are an essential ingredient of higher education, and the role of money is often an important gauge of a church's involvement in its college. Of crucial importance in Calvin's history is the CRC policy of assessing all congregations for denominational causes and agencies.[11] In 1884, for example, the 59 congregations were each assessed an annual quota, ranging from $240 from the Spring Street Church in Grand Rapids to $6 from the Oost Vriesland (Iowa) congregation. For many years these quotas formed a major

11 See Ryskamp, *Offering Hearts,* chap. 22 for details on this "quota" support.

percentage of Calvin's income.[12] Indeed, there was an initial reluctance to accept any funding from outside the CRC, since such funding would loosen the bond between church and school. When the administration wanted to launch a Million Dollar Endowment Fund, Classis Sioux Center demurred, because the school might become too independent, and "our Christian Reformed people will no longer experience the bond with the College" (*Agenda for Synod* 1920, vii). In later financial campaigns, the Christian Reformed people proved themselves extremely generous in the support of the school. (CRC students have benefited from this generosity, since they pay less tuition than non-CRC students.)

One complication in this support has been the location of the college. From the beginning there were those who looked upon Calvin as a regional school and considered it unfair that folks in New Jersey and Minnesota were expected to support a Michigan college. After the establishment of colleges by CRC members in Iowa, Illinois, Ontario, and Alberta, the obligatory support of Calvin continued to rankle distant supporters. Since 1963 the quotas have been prorated; churches near other CRC-related colleges were permitted to decrease their quota—on the assumption that they would support Dordt College or one of the other regional colleges.

Another financial complication arose out of the responsibility-control dynamics discussed above. CRC supporters felt that since they founded Calvin College, established it as a (Christian) Reformed institution, supported it sacrificially, they should also be able to control it. And one way of controlling a college is to control the flow of funds. This control became a major issue, especially in the 1980s and 1990s. Since they did not approve of student behavior or

[12] This percentage has decreased sharply over the years. The percentage for selected years is as follows: 1945: 64%; 1955: 51%; 1975: 24% (certain regions with other "CRC colleges" could now decrease their Calvin quota); 1995: 4.8% (after the college and seminary had separated). Quota support is not the only indicator of CRC support, but it is significant.

faculty teachings, individual donors and congregations sometimes threatened to withdraw support and many actually cut off funds.

Synod and Board of Trustees

Another way of measuring the close relationship between church and school is to look at the church's involvement in the administration of the college, especially through synodical decisions. A few examples will illustrate this involvement. In 1896, synod determined that the school was to give an exact account of the income and expenditures of each fund. This practice has continued throughout the college's history. The "exact account" may not be as minute as it once was, but the "College Report to Synod 1999" still dutifully included a summary of the operating budget. In 1947, the board announced to synod that it planned to purchase an electric mimeograph, and in 1951 it recommended "that Synod approve the setting up of the Library Reference service." A college catalog was not published till 1907; previous to that time the catalog information was recorded in the *Acts of Synod*. Until 1993, synod approved the appointment of every new professor, including one-year appointments and visiting professors, and the tenure appointment of each professor still has to be ratified by synod. Moreover, major building projects have always been approved by synod. The most direct synodical control occurred in 1939-1940, when the Committee of Ten, appointed by synod, arrogated much power in its attempt to cleanse the college of un-Reformed teaching and questionable conduct.

One indicator of synodical involvement is the "Index to Synodical Decisions, 1857-1980." Calvin is among the longest catalog of items in this listing. Again, the decisions range widely, from the number of hours of Dutch required for preseminary students, to faculty pensions, to a discussion about a Calvinistic university.

In recent decades synodical supervision has decreased. Beginning in the 1950s the trustees report to synod increased the section, "For Information," and reduced the section, "Recommendations," considerably. Nevertheless, each synod is still asked to approve new academic programs, to elect every board member, and to approve the budget.

As in most North American colleges and universities, the Calvin College Board of Trustees plays a prominent role. At the official founding of the school, the synod minutes record rather offhandedly: "The matter came up that the school needs a Curatorium to have oversight of the same, and that one of those appointed must serve as treasurer" (*Acts*, 1876, Art. 30). Four ministers were appointed, with the mandate to meet once a year to keep an eye on the school. That modest assemblage grew into a governing body that became a crucial link between church and school. In 1878, the school was incorporated, requiring the appointment of trustees.[13]

Board members were elected from each classis and then approved by synod. The curators and board members worked tirelessly for the college, made thousands of small and large decisions, appropriated millions of dollars, observed the professors in the classroom, tried to explain the college to the church constituency (not always succeeding), and sought to maintain the dream of the founders.[14]

Their work was not always appreciated. The church at times felt that the board ought to be more firm with those professors in Grand Rapids. The professors often thought that the board meddled in educational matters about which they knew very little. Students generally ignored the board, unless the trustees tried to clip student wings. Author Peter De Vries found early local renown because of his tussle with the board When the curatorium (trustees) did not acquiesce with a student proposal to institute an organization fee, De Vries wrote (in)famously in the opening sentence of his

[13] Originally the curators dealt mostly with educational matters, and the trustees with legal and business issues. However, these lines of responsibility were often stretched, and there was overlap in membership and duties. For a time there also was a Curatorium Contractum, which consisted of curators from Michigan and Illinois. By the mid-1930s the Curatorium and the Board of Trustees appear to have merged.

[14] The most thorough study of the role of the Board of Trustees is by Bernard Pekelder, "The Role of the Board of Trustees in Operating a Church-Related College: A Case Study" (M.A. Thesis, Northwestern University, 1965).

editorial: "Now that our frail hopes have been championed before that august assembly which pursues the agenda between huge draughts of Java and stern circumnavigation around the perimeters of doughnuts, and now that they have been duly blasted to atoms of smithereens by the roaring artillery of mustered dogma and by the noise of theological shrapnel, the student leaders of Calvin College can proceed on the perennial course of competitive begging." For good measure he then called them "a very pious or very lazy Curatorium" and "this vest pocket edition of the Sanhedrin."[15] In later years, the board again crossed swords with the *Chimes*, as the constituency took umbrage with articles and editorials.[16]

Relations between the board and the faculty were at times strained, but overall the board has been supportive (or at least tolerant) of faculty. The longest controversy was about the faculty's supervision (or lack thereof) of students attending movies. Pekelder speaks of "an almost unending tension between Board and faculty."[17] No doubt the curatorium of 1930 (and all other trustees) deserved better press than De Vries accorded them! As we shall see in chapter 6, the board was often caught between a very conservative constituency and a more progressive campus. By and large they deserve accolades for their 125-year reign.

Finally, one indication of the "churchiness" of the board is its ministerial membership. Although the question of having lay people on the board was discussed as early as 1922, it was not till 1948 that the first non-clergy were added. The first woman board member was elected in 1976; the first non-CRC members were admitted in 1992.

Faculty

Calvin faculty members represented a very strong link to the church. The early appointees to the Theological School were nearly

15 *Chimes*, October 17, 1930, p. 2.
16 See Pekelder, "Role of the Board," 103-109.
17 Pekelder, p. 91.

all CRC ministers, and from the beginning of the college all professors were members of the CRC. In 1892 synod had stipulated that when an appointee "accepts the nomination, he shall, if he is not a member, become a member of the Dutch Christian Reformed Church." In addition to becoming a member of a local CRC congregation, the new professor also was asked to sign the "Formula of Subscription." The "Formula" states that the signer agrees with the doctrines of the CRC as they are expressed in the "Three Forms of Unity"—The Belgic Confession, the Heidelberg Catechism, and the Canons of Dordt (*Acts of Synod* 1892, Supplement 6, Art. 4). This stipulation was extended to the college faculty as well and firmly adhered to. But at times the board agonized about having to engage "outsiders" for some part-time positions. In 1925, "approval is given to the appointment of a leader of the orchestra not connected with our church, but as soon as a man from our circles can be found, the appointment ceases."[18]

There is no record of a college professor coming from "outside" and joining the CRC before 1954. At that time Charles Miller came as a visiting professor and was tendered a regular appointment in 1956. By then he had joined the CRC, and the board minutes explain that the original appointment "was conditional because of his lack of orientation in our group" (May, 1956, art. 68). Similarly, in 1965 a candidate did not receive a regular appointment, because "Mr. Marsden is presently a member of the Orthodox Presbyterian Church which is the reason for the 'Visiting' status" (BOT Minutes, Feb. 11, 1965, art. 39). Since then many other faculty from outside the CRC have joined the Calvin faculty. In 1970, approximately 18 faculty out of a total of 174 were not CRC members at the time of their appointments; in 1999, there were 115 out of 319. All of these, with a few exceptions, joined the CRC. The membership requirement was reiterated in 1974, in a trustees document "Tenure at Calvin." The church requirement became somewhat broadened in 1993,

[18] Quoted in ibid., 62.

when faculty could join denominations "in ecclesiastical fellowship" with the CRC. In 2000, the only such denomination with congregations in Grand Rapids (where faculty might attend) is the RCA.[19]

Students

Students were a crucial link with the church, since both the Literary Department and later the college program were established for CRC youth. Although from the beginning some CRC young people attended colleges other than Calvin (a practice often frowned upon), the standard educational route was Christian elementary and high school, capped by enrollment at Calvin College. This decades-long procession of students who became alumni helped enormously to strengthen the bond between school and church.

This arrangement, however, became complicated by two developments. First, with the establishment of other CRC-related colleges after 1955, the number of CRC students from states and provinces outside of Michigan decreased substantially. For example, the combined enrollment of Dordt, Trinity, Kings, and Redeemer colleges in 1999 was approximately 3,500, of whom 53 percent were from CRC homes. Thus the potential pool of students to Calvin decreased, and loyalty to Calvin was diluted.

Secondly, since admission to Calvin never was restricted to CRC members, students from other denominations and those without church affiliation began to attend. It appears that in most years statistics were kept for denominational affiliation, but these numbers were often not recorded in the reports to board or synod, and the earlier years are therefore not available. The following chart shows the CRC membership percentages at approximately five-year intervals. (I was not able to locate figures for some years.)

[19] See chapter 8 for further discussion of this issue.

YEAR	% of CRC STUDENTS	TOTAL ENROLLMENT
1932	81	393
1935	75	400
1940	86	499
1947	87	1395
1950	86	1270
1955	89	1541
1960	90	2232
1966	93	3234
1970		3437
1975	83	3674
1980	77	4108
1985	71	4053
1990	64	4270
1995	59	3963
1999	54	4273

The college's stance toward such students has often been ambivalent. Certainly those students' tuition was a welcome addition to the coffers, and besides, the teaching of the college would be a wholesome influence for the outsiders. At the same time, the influence of the non-CRC students upon the CRC youth was considered dangerous. I found the most extended discussion on this issue in 1936. The minutes of the board record the following: "The Executive Committee's report touched the question of having students at our institution who are not Christian Reformed. This led to a long discussion in which it appears that there are many angles which have to be considered. . . . The Board decides to inform Synod that both the Faculty and the Board of Trustees are alive to the danger created by the presence of these students, and are constantly and seriously struggling with this problem" (Art. 36). The *Agenda to Synod* of that same year included a letter written by two concerned constituents who voiced similar apprehensions and added: This situation "encourages courtship of our own students with young folks who do not stand for the faith of the fathers" (*Agenda*, Part II, 441). I suppose Calvin and the CRC were not very different from other religious/ethnic subcultures in trying to maintain doctrinal/ecclesiastical purity, but the general attitude to "outsiders" shows a lamentable narrowness. (In 1934 the president came to the magnanimous conclusion that "some of our own students, coming from various sections of the country, cause us greater concern than those few outsiders").[20]

Fortunately, such negative attitudes toward outsiders did change. Over the years, membership in the CRC became less important, and recruitment in high schools other than schools associated with Christian Schools International more common. The desire for greater ethnic diversity also played a role. In 1985 the college developed a strategy with the imposing title, "The Comprehensive Plan for Integrating North American Ethnic Minority Persons and their Interests into every Facet of Calvin's Institutional Life." Although the strategy for recruiting more minority persons did not necessarily imply the enrollment of more non-CRC students, in reality the increase of minority persons does involve major recruitment outside the CRC. The statistics above clearly indicate that, in terms of student body, Calvin has greatly broadened its ecclesiastical base.

Calvin has always shown the same concern for the students' spiritual welfare, as do other Christian colleges. Chapel services have always been a part of campus life (with compulsory versus voluntary chapel attendance debated for years), and the college has consistently encouraged Bible study and prayer groups, as well as volunteerism and outreach to the community. What has distinguished Calvin as a CRC institution have been several emphases. One has been the concern for the students' continued attendance in CRC congregations and the accompanying supervision of the students' spiritual life by a local council or consistory. At various times the college required the students to join a local CR congregation, or

20 President's Report to the BOT, 5.

recommended a "student membership" in such churches, or sought to have campus worship services under the supervision of local consistories.

As we will see in chapter 6, the constituency also took a strong interest in student (mis)behavior. Here too, CRC mores came to expression. Whereas in many conservative Christian colleges the issue of drinking alcohol was of paramount importance, at Calvin that issue was not addressed very frequently by parents. The administration of the college was probably more concerned about drinking problems than the constituency. President Schulze commented: "Our people, as far as I know, have never committed themselves to the position of a 'teetotaler.' A 'slokje' now and then is regarded as permissible. [But] there is a dangerous potential here."[21]

Instead, the major discipline issue for forty years, and the most vociferous criticism by the church, was on the matter of "worldly amusement," especially movie theater attendance. Another issue of student behavior that marked the college as CRC was smoking among women. Whereas men (both faculty and students) had always smoked pipe, cigar, and cigarette like the proverbial chimneys, for years the dean of women faithfully recorded her battles against "smoking by the girls."

In the Family

In addition to CRC involvement in Calvin College via finances, legal ownership, faculty, students, and mores, one finds an even more pervasive sense of "familial" ownership. Calling Calvin College "our school" (earlier: *onze school*) might at times become a slogan, useful when trying to persuade the CRC constituency to contribute (once again) to the support of Calvin, but the description was more than a slogan.

In the Calvin College and Seminary *Semi-Centennial Volume, 1876-1926*, the phrase "our school" appears on virtually every page.

21 Report to BOT, Feb. 1949, p. 8.

Throughout the years there was a deep sense of ownership and pride in Calvin. *The Banner*, the English denominational periodical, carried a weekly column about the school for years, with items ranging from the names of soloists in the Calvin chapel, to the announcement that the college's financial secretary had suffered an apoplectic stroke, to a lucid explanation of the integration of faith and learning. Frequently the Calvin College and Seminary reports and decisions at the annual synods took more time and space than that of any other church agency or department. Consistories discussed the potential appointment of a new Bible professor heatedly and knowledgeably.

In my final chapter I will more fully assess the strengths and weaknesses, the pros and cons of the church-college relationship. Let me touch on a few issues here. Calvin College has grown from very humble beginnings to a premier Christian college, recognized in both Christian circles and the wider academic community. Its leadership in the Council of Christian College and Universities is unparalleled; in the past twenty-five years Calvin has been able to model the integration of faith and learning and the promotion of a "Christian mind" in Christian higher education. One can only speculate, of course, whether the insights and tradition developed at Calvin could have arisen if Calvin had been an "independent" school. It appears to me that the confessional ties to the CRC and the inheritance of the Calvinistic-Kuyperian foundation have been largely responsible for nurturing Calvin College's intellectual and spiritual direction. What has been the benefit to the church? An educated clergy, a sturdy tradition of theologically aware lay people, a refusal to capitulate to either fundamentalism or liberalism, a balance between word and deed ministry—these features of the CRC were strengthened by the theological and intellectual leadership of Calvin College.[22]

[22] The best recent exploration of the relationship between college and church can be found in the pamphlet "An Expanded Statement of the Mission of Calvin College: Vision, Purpose, Commitment" (1996), especially 19-29.

As suggested by some of the previous discussion and statistics, the relationship between Calvin College and the CRC has undergone considerable change. Whereas fifty years ago, trustees and faculty were all members of the CRC, as were about 90 percent of the student body, by the year 2000 this had changed dramatically. The board now includes non-CRC members, a third of the faculty was non-CRC when hired, and nearly one-half of the student body is from "outside." The assessed quota support from each CRC congregation at one time accounted for 65 percent of Calvin's total income; today it is less than 5 percent. The challenge for the future is to discern how church and school can best continue the relationship in a way that will strengthen both the denomination and the college.

Excursus: Hope College

In this study I have not attempted to compare Calvin College explicitly to other colleges. However, such comparisons would be very enlightening. Let me briefly suggest how a comparative look at Hope College would be especially instructive.[23]

Hope College came out of the same milieu as Calvin College. The Dutch Reformed immigrant community that gave rise to Calvin also created Hope. Soon after the 1857 split between the RCA and the CRC, the RCA started Hope. The school was begun as a preparatory school for seminary study and by 1866 it matured into a college. The growth of Hope through the years has largely paralleled Calvin, with very similar academic programs and close ties to its sponsoring denomination. The schools have at times been competitive (not the least on the basketball court) but have also sought cooperation.

However, there have also been significant differences in their development. One difference lies in the number of RCA schools. Two Iowa colleges, Central College in Pella and Northwestern

23 Two helpful titles on Hope's history and identity are Gordon Van Wylen, *Vision for a Christian College* (Grand Rapids: Eerdmans, 1988), and Wynand Wichers, *A Century of Hope, 1866-1966* (Grand Rapids: Eerdmans, 1968).

College in Orange City, are on a par with Hope in their church affiliation, whereas Calvin has always been the only official denominational school, with other CRC-supported colleges (Dordt, Trinity, Redeemer, Kings) having no such status. Today the RCA and its colleges have a "Covenant of Mutual Responsibilities" that is much more "loose" than the relationship between Calvin and the CRC.

The church affiliation of professors is also significantly different. At no time did Hope require its faculty to be (or become) members of the RCA. At one time, professors were required to sign the Form of Subscription to the Reformed confessions, but that was discontinued in the mid-1970s. Today the faculty includes members of many Protestant denominations, as well as the Roman Catholic and Greek Orthodox churches.

The student body has also been more varied. In 2000, the percentage of RCA students is only 22 percent, and the second largest group of students is Roman Catholic.

The long struggle of Calvin in determining its identity as an American institution had no counterpart at Hope. Since the nineteenth-century immigrants joined the RCA, with its three hundred years of American history, its identity with the Netherlands and with Dutch Reformed traditions was much less pronounced. Its identification with American culture and academic life was therefore greatly accelerated.

Hope's identity as a Christian college has also been very different from Calvin's. The neo-Calvinistic influence of Abraham Kuyper was largely absent, and the models of the North American Christian college more influential. The mission of Hope College has therefore been interpreted much more diversely than Calvin's.

This brief sketch of the history and identity of Hope College suggests that a thorough study of Hope's church relationship and its identity as a Christian college would be highly desirable and rewarding. Such a profile would complement this study of the relationship between Calvin College and the CRC.

5

"What's the Matter with Calvin?"

As indicated earlier, the relationship between Calvin and the CRC has been complex, and it has included a great variety of critical voices. Some of the critics were faithful supporters of the college who merely protested a particular foible, such as the showing of *Clockwork Orange.* Others saw Calvin on the proverbial slippery slope—either near the top or close to the bottom. Still others called the college "apostate." The criticisms ran the gamut from students wearing "barefoot sandals" at a worship service, to the introduction of square dance, to the teaching of evolution, to the posture toward "secular" scholarship. One thread that appears over and over again is the concern about the Christian's (and therefore the church's or college's) relationship to "the world." The biblical "being in but not of the world" is, of course, a crucial ingredient of the Christian life, and both the CRC and Calvin have sought (and continue to seek) the demarcations between God's kingdom and the kingdom of darkness.

To some readers the review and analysis of the various critiques of Calvin College may not seem either necessary or edifying. However, the censure of Calvin is an essential part of its history and deserves to be told. More importantly, each criticism and Calvin's response helped to define the nature of the college and its relationship to the CRC. For example, the 1936 synod's concern that the college accepted too many "outside" students prompted Calvin to consider its mission in terms of admissions, both at that time and later. The same was true of the controversies about theater attendance and films, worship on and off campus, speakers whose views and lectures were opposed to Christian (Reformed) views, and the development (or lack thereof) of Christian scholarship. These and dozens of other issues compelled the college to deliberate about its identity, its task, and its place in the CRC (and to develop a public relations office!).

The Criticism

The title of this chapter is borrowed from a 1921 editorial title in *The Banner.*[1] Editor Henry Beets asked that question after he had heard widespread criticism of the college. His editorial proceeded to look at some of the charges and he generally defended the Calvin, even though he also had some words of reproof. The question, "What's the Matter with Calvin?" has often been posed, and not all who asked it have been as generous as Beets. Three historians of Calvin College have sought to analyze the conflicts that sometimes simmered, sometimes flared up between the college and the CRC.

George Stob, in his doctoral dissertation, devotes a substantial chapter to this issue. He finds the first major criticism arising after World War I, both because the times were unsettling and because the college had outgrown its infancy stage. Stob then summarizes a skirmish between two (unrelated) Kuipers: H.J. Kuiper, editor of *The Witness* (a conservative CRC journal), and B.K. Kuiper, editor of *De Wachter* (the denominational Dutch-language magazine). HJK assailed the college for losing its Reformed distinctiveness, being more interested in academic excellence than Calvinistic teaching, inviting non-Christian speakers to campus, allowing

[1] November 1, 1921, 724-25.

choirs to sing non-Christian songs, and in general disappointing its constituency. BKK accused HJK of unfairly agitating against the college, advocating a hot-house education (where one might just as well take all non-Reformed books out of the library), and being more Anabaptist than Reformed.[2] Stob interprets the controversy largely in terms of disagreement on how the Christian and a Christian college ought to relate to the world, both in terms of conduct and scholarship.

Henry Ryskamp, in *Offering Hearts, Shaping Lives,* traces the criticism launched at the college over the years. For example, Ryskamp sums up the reaction to the writings in the progressive *Reformed Journal* (most of which were authored by Calvin professors), as follows:

> Criticism came not only from the editor of *The Banner* but also from the editor and associate editors of *Torch and Trumpet.* The soundness of the theological and philosophical views of the *Reformed Journal* writers have been repeatedly challenged by the critics. As a consequence of the situation caused by the writings and speeches of the *Reformed Journal* editors, a small group of men, very conservative critics, have set themselves up as defenders of the faith and have not only severely criticized what has been said and written but have also on occasion called for retraction, or else! One can imagine what this might do to the peace and serenity of the atmosphere in the church. Critics have asked the board and the synod to investigate. At times it has seemed as if there might be another schism in the denomination.[3]

He then commiserates with the lot of President Spoelhof:

> Also during his administration, students, aroused by debates carried on in church papers, aroused by the conflict in the

[2] See George Stob, "The Christian Reformed Church and Her Schools," especially pp. 356-71, for complete citations.
[3] Ryskamp, *Offering Hearts*, 188.

> political, economic, and social arenas in this country, frequently give utterance to ideas which, to conservative critics, confirm their suspicions that there is something wrong at Calvin College. Telephone calls, denunciatory letters, articles in the church papers critical of the faculty and the students come so often as to make a sensitive person wonder whether the attempt is worthwhile to head up a Calvinistic institution and to assist not only in the perpetuation of the truly Reformed position but to reshape it honestly and boldly, to make it relevant and challenging to the modern world.[4]

Ryskamp's analysis of the opposition is similar to Stob's. The confrontations between the college and many in the church was occasioned largely by the different visions of how the Reformed heritage should function in a new world. Ryskamp defends the college by positing that contemporary philosophical, social, economic, and scientific views and situations demand more than a mere repetition of old slogans.

John Timmerman sounds a note similar to Stob and Ryskamp in his history. His final chapter, "Little Foxes in the Vineyard," focuses on a number of skirmishes between school and church.

> From that year [1918] to this [1976] Calvin has rarely been free from suspicion, mistrust, and attack. Few colleges have been more sedulously observed; whenever the torch flickered or somebody thought it did, the trumpet was sounded. Throughout these many years, in mild or vehement ways, the college has been criticized for not being sufficiently aggressive in pulverizing apostasy, for failing to be distinctively or creatively Reformed, for keeping a loose rein on worldliness, for advancing radical ideas or for not advancing them. No facet of college life has escaped: neither the first administration nor the last, nor any in

[4] Ibid., 189.

> between; neither the faculty or the student body whether in the statement of opinion or action. All have been assailed more often on the basis of rumor than reality. The criticism has originated in concern and love, but also in hot temper and prejudice.[5]

Timmerman deals largely with reactions against student and faculty writing but recognizes a more general animosity as well. In some ways he considers the strife unavoidable: "As long as Calvin is supported by a constituency composed of pietistic elements who suspect learning, traditionalists who insist on doctrinal purity, and Kuyperians of one kind or another, who emphasize creative development and cultural engagement, and as long as the college stresses loyalty to Reformed perspectives, there will be tension about what the 'absolute Lordship of Christ' implies in an educational institution."[6]

All three authors suggest that Calvin College has received more bellicose treatment than other church colleges. I will leave it to students of education history to judge whether Calvin indeed did fare worse than other schools in relation to its constituency. Certainly the examples cited by Stob, Ryskamp, and Timmerman, as well as chapters 6 and 7 in this work, demonstrate that alumni and church members scrutinized the college very closely and were more than ready to pounce on any perceived collegiate negligence or heresy.

No doubt the critics of Calvin considered their critique a God-given obligation to wage war on departures from the truth and from the Christian (Reformed) walk. However, it is difficult to avoid the impression that a spirit of quarrelsomeness also played a role. Why the frequently harsh criticism? The controversies in the history of the CRC and of Calvin College may have arisen partly out of the church's origin. The denomination originated from three church splits (the 1834 and 1886 secessions in the Netherlands, and the

[5] Timmerman, *Promises*, 175.
[6] Ibid., 193.

1857 separation from the Reformed Church in America). Another church split occurred in 1924, with the origin of the Protestant Reformed Churches. Such secessions sharpen theological sensitivity and judgment, and the CRC has always been zealous for doctrinal purity. However, this history also has a less admirable outcome—the search for truth may become little more than a habit of theological wrangling and bickering. This habit carried over in the church's relationship to Calvin: the search for doctrinal purity played a role, but so did personality clashes, power struggles, and nitpicking squabbles.

Combined with this history is the sense of ownership discussed earlier. The constituency argued that since Calvin College is "our school," and we pay for its operation, especially through the required quotas, then we have a right to be upset if professors promote strange teachings and students go barefoot . Moreover, for many years of its existence, a large number of the college's supporters had received only secondary education (at times only elementary); their notion of education often differed from what actually occurs in academia. The constituency sometimes had little patience with professors' scientific inquiries or new conclusions, nor with students' tendency to rebel against tradition.

Did (do) these Dutch Calvinist immigrants also possess a particularly spiteful streak in their collective psyche? I will not attempt to psychoanalyze 150 years of an ethnic population. Instead, let me cite the Reverend Izerd Van Dellen, a long-time minister in the CRC, who did analyze the "character" of CRC folks in a lecture at the fiftieth anniversary of the denomination. First he pays tribute to the laudable characteristics, such as steadiness, thoroughness, solidness, cleanliness, determination, truthfulness, honesty. But then Van Dellen adds the "dark side":

> After arrival in the new world...one finds a strain of narrow-mindedness in our character...and excessive isolation. Caution at times became suspicion and distrust. We were not free from arrogance. Frequently our

> environment and new situations were judged unfairly and with a sense of superiority. This was shown, for example, in the despising by many of the English language. At times people wanted to maintain the old ways just because they were old: it's always been that way and it should stay that way.[7]

It is noteworthy that Van Dellen attributes some of these traits to arriving in the new world. No doubt the experience of emigration is a potent force in shaping a community—emigration often presses people into a defensive posture. Such defensiveness no doubt has left its imprint on the history of the CRC.

Competing Emphases

To fully understand the dynamics of Calvin-CRC relations we must also try to disentangle some of the ideological streams and directions in the CRC. For our purpose the streams in the CRC can be labeled *Pietist*, *Confessionalist*, and *Kuyperian.*

Pietists stress a life of devotion and personal holiness, as it comes to expression in a close walk with the Lord. Such a walk will emphasize prayer, spirituality, Bible study, as well as a pure life that avoids worldly entanglements. This stream was in strong evidence in the 1834 Secession in the Netherlands and continued in the CRC, where it became nourished by American fundamentalism. *Confessionalists* emphasize the doctrinal life of the church. Their stance includes strict fidelity to the church's historic creeds, wariness about new theological developments, and militancy about maintaining traditions. This stream also came as an inheritance from the Reformed Churches in the Netherlands and became a hallmark of the CRC (note the subtitle of John Kromminga's book, *The Christian Reformed Church: A Study in Orthodoxy*). *Kuyperians* stress

[7] Izerd Van Dellen, "Het Karakter van ons Volk naar Schaduw-en Lichtzijden," in *Gedenkboek van het Vijtigjarig Jubileum de Christelijke Gereformeerde Kerk,*. 2 nd ed. (Grand Rapids: Semi-Centennial Committee, 1907), 194.

the importance of the Christian's participation in all of life, citing the "cultural mandate" to be involved in God's creation and world. All followers of Kuyper agree on that cultural responsibility, but they often go different directions; they tend to emphasize either one of Abraham Kuyper's leading principles—the antithesis or common grace. Those who focus on the antithesis are apt to see the secularism in modern life and therefore the need for transforming culture, perhaps through separate organizations. For example, all Kuyperians have recognized that labor relations need Christian leavening; the antithetical Kuyperians have sought to do so by advocating separate Christian labor organizations in opposition to secular labor unions. Common grace advocates are more receptive to the notion of God's gifts to humanity, and they stress that the "natural light" in all people allows us to be grateful recipients of truth and beauty wherever we find it. For example, we may challenge some of the suppositions of Plato or William Wordsworth, but we can also learn much from them. Calvin College has always carried the torch for Kuyperianism (the obligation to be involved in cultural affairs)—sometimes stressing the antithesis, sometimes common grace.

As soon as I have drawn up this CRC categorization I must, of course, apologize for it! It is hardly a neat taxonomy. There are no pure types of any of these groups, and one person may well be intensely pious, thoroughly Reformed in doctrine, and an ardent transformer of culture. Moreover, as various authors or theologians banded together into alliances (for example, in *The Reformed Journal*, or the Association of Christian Reformed Laymen, or the Association for the Advancement of Christian Studies) there was constant fluidity in these alliances. To complicate the taxonomy even more, since the CRC was an immigrant denomination, the issue of Americanization flows through all of these ideological eddies and tributaries, with each group containing partisans for greater or lesser acceptance of American culture. Again, these streams are not to be seen as factions that were always in competition for the soul of the denomination. Often these emphases were in creative tension, and igniting a dynamic energy in the denomination.

However, at other times one does see rivalry between these forces, and for the analysis of the relationship between Calvin College and the CRC, the categorization of pietists, confessionalists, and Kuyperians will often be a helpful delineation for our understanding. (In some instances I will combine the pietists and ponfessionalists into one category of traditionalists/conservatives, in their common critique of Calvin).[8]

The Critics

As noted above, censure of the college came from a wide array of sources and a large number of people. To have a more complete picture of the college-church relationship it will be helpful to identify some specific critics. We will look at two very different organizations to illustrate the complexity of Calvin's place in the CRC.

The Association of Christian Reformed Laymen. One of the staunchest critics of Calvin College was the Association of Christian Reformed Laymen (ACRL). The ACRL was begun in 1965 to engage in "a more positive, militant, and timely defense of the Reformed faith" in the CRC.[9] But one of its first circulars, sent out to "Dear Brethren in the Lord," stated an additional purpose: "The ACRL has come into being because of disturbing voices which have been raised out of Calvin College...."[10] The ACRL *News Bulletin* first appeared in October 1968 and continued to appear till April 1981 (No. 92). This final issue noted that the "creeping modernism [of

8 For greater refinement and elaboration of these categories see the following: Henry Stob on three "minds" in the CRC: *The Reformed Journal*, March, April, July-August, October, 1957; Henry Zwaanstra, *Reformed Thought and Experience in a New World* (Kampen, Kok, 1973), esp. chap. 3; Nicholas Wolterstorff, "The AACS in the CRC," *Reformed Journal*, December, 1974, 9-16; James Bratt, *Dutch Calvinism in Modern America*, esp. chaps. 3 and 4.

9 "Preamble of the Constitution and By-laws of the Association of Christian Reformed Laymen."

10 Circular dated February 8, 1965.

the 1960s] has become a stream that has engulfed the entire CRC under the direction of the Seminary." A thorough consideration of the role of the ACRL in the CRC would be enlightening, but in this study I will limit myself to the association's involvement with Calvin College. The best way to capture both the issues that troubled the ACRL, and the tone in which they delivered their criticism, is by quoting from their *News Bulletin.*

What were the issues that most troubled the ACRL? The worship life of Calvin students was of great concern. One manifestation of things gone wrong was the college's involvement in an "underground church." These were experimental services (initially conducted at the LaGrave Avenue Christian Reformed Church) characterized by informal style, casual dress, and guitar accompaniment. Although Calvin never officially sponsored these services, Calvin College was apparently involved: "Dr. Wolterstorff and Dr. Orlebeke of Calvin College staff were very much in evidence at this meeting....at this disgraceful event....We could weep when we see Calvin students being fed stones instead of bread."[11]

President Spoelhof and chaplain Bernard Pekelder rebutted these and later charges with a forceful letter, sent to all CRC ministers and councils (dated Dec. 18, 1969), blasting the ACRL for its tactics ("this denominational bearing of false witness is damaging to ministers of the Gospel and is a sin") and explaining the true nature of those services. In a subsequent *Bulletin*[12] the scene deteriorated into tragicomedy, as the ACRL writers (never signing their articles) denounced Spoelhof and Pekelder and described the ejecting of the uninvited editor of the *Chimes* from an ACRL meeting.

Similar criticism was voiced about worship services held on campus. One *Bulletin* was wholly devoted to the rhetorical question, "You Call This Worship?" Both the leadership of the college (especially chaplain Pekelder) and the services were lambasted. The

[11] *News Bulletin,* No. 2, December, 1968. The authors of the articles were not named.
[12] *News Bulletin,* No. 10, January, 1970.

use of rock music, liturgical dance, trendy liturgies, off-beat sermons—all were met with the challenge: "Surely it is time that the laymen of the Christian Reformed Church rise up and demand a purge of these evils."[13]

Other happenings at Calvin also received appraisal. Art professor Robert Jensen's cartoons were announced with suspicion: "IS THIS CHRISTIAN ART?"[14] The appearance of speakers such as Father Groppi, Malcolm Boyd, and Martin Marty was greeted with, "What will you say? How long will you pay?"[15] When Calvin played an audio performance of *Jesus Christ, Superstar*, the *News Bulletin* judged, "We stand in amazement that, what we consider the works of the devil, should be brought into the very bosom of Calvin College and fed to our covenant youth."[16] Another issue was devoted to the approval of "social dancing" at Calvin. This evil was the "last straw," and the ACRL recommended the withholding of financial support, especially via the quota system—the annual assessment of congregations and families.[17] In its final issue the ACRL took a final shot at Calvin, citing the "systematic deception practiced by both the College and the Seminary faculties during the past decade....Calvin College has become a hotbed of the so-called 'new left' (warmed over socialism) and liberation theology."[18]

The ACRL was the most combative organization assailing Calvin College. Its members constituted the "far right" of the conservative wing of the CRC, representing both the pietist and the confessional tradition. They spread the news about Calvin in the denomination, first by reprinting brochures, clippings from the Calvin *Chimes* and other papers, synod reports, liturgies from worship services, communications by the Calvin administration, and protest letters sent to Calvin by constituents. At times these citations and reprintings

13 *News Bulletin,* No. 24, June, 1971.
14 *News Bulletin,* No. 14, July, 1970.
15 *News Bulletin,* No. 13, May, 1970.
16 *News Bulletin,* No. 22, April, 1971.
17 *News Bulletin,* No. 81, February, 1978.
18 *News Bulletin,* No. 92, April, 1981.

presented an accurate portrayal of "what goes on at Calvin"; more often they were quotations out of context. Second, they editorialized about the college, as shown by some of the citations above. The overall effect was a "demonizing" of Calvin College. The board, administration, and faculty were accused, at best, of moral neglect and betrayal of the heritage of church and school; at worst, the school was portrayed as a hotbed of heresy and apostasy. The students were seen as either dupes of the malicious faculty or as perpetrators of modern decadence.

The Association for the Advancement of Christian Studies

The relationship between Calvin College and the Association for the Advancement of Christian Scholarship (AACS), in the context of the CRC, is a complicated one. The institutional connections were complex, since both Calvin and the AACS were largely located within the CRC constituency, Calvin as a denominational school, the AACS as an independent association and later as the Institute for Christian Studies (ICS). Calvin was sometimes at odds with a segment of the denomination, and so was the AACS—but the lines of allegiances and opposition were very fluid. The issues were also complex. They included the role of the Canadian section of the CRC, the payment of quotas, theological questions about the Word of God, and philosophical issues, such as the views of the Dutch philosopher Herman Dooyeweerd, the principal sage of the AACS.[19] I will try to tease out some of the matters most relevant to our discussion.

First, a few comments about history and context. As mentioned earlier, the Dutch immigrants who came to Canada and joined the CRC had received a continuing exposure to the influence of Abraham Kuyper and had lived in a Reformed community in which Calvinism found expression in all manner of Christian (that is,

19 Dooyeweerd developed a Christian (that is, Calvinistic) philosophy that sought to be sharply different from all non-Christian philosophies. He criticized Roman Catholic views as synthesis philosophies.

Reformed) organizations in the Netherlands. From schools to newspapers, from labor unions to goat breeding societies, from political parties to gymnastics clubs—these were linked into a staunch Calvinistic subculture in the Netherlands.

There were various attempts to transplant the seeds of this history into North American (especially Canadian) soil. Christian journalism, labor organization, farmers federation, and schools were established with more or less success. Christian schools received special attention and were founded at great financial sacrifice. And the dream of a Christian, a Reformed, university was not long in coming. In 1956 the Association for Reformed Scientific Studies (later: AACS) was founded, with the ultimate goal of founding a Calvinistic University. The dream began to take shape with a series of annual summer lectures in Unionville, Ontario, and with the establishment of the Institute for Christian Studies in 1967, in Toronto.

The relationship of this movement to Calvin College was often strained. Many of the adherents of the AACS had no academic or family connection to Calvin and thus no alumni loyalty. Others, including students at the college, were also very censorious. The criticism of Calvin College was expressed especially by those who had identified themselves with the campus "Groen Club" (named after the Christian statesman in the Netherlands, Guillaume Groen van Prinsterer). One example can be found in a letter by John Vander Stelt to his CRC home church in Brantford, Ontario. Vander Stelt had just been graduated from Calvin, was headed for the Free University in Amsterdam, and later became a strong proponent of the AACS. He had this to say about his alma mater:

> Calvin College is a well that is becoming polluted with liberalism....The instruction we as students receive in psychology, sociology, politics, partly in history, English, and philosophy is not distinctively Christian at all. [Switching to Dutch, he continues.] There is a lack of deeply-grounded Christian scholarship....One hears definitions of culture,

> religion, faith, reason, psychology, history, philosophy, etc. that are not Reformed or Biblical, but are saturated with the products and spirit of a secularized, semi-Roman Catholic scholarship.[20]

Calvin Seerveld, another graduate of Calvin College who became associated with the AACS, was caught by a "spiritual force" during his college career. What was this force? "One unholy spirit which has captivated Christian education again and again...: the appealing, respectable, vitiating spirit of Christian accommodation to the traditions of men..., a tempting synthesizing perspective...."[21]

A pivotal figure in this history was H. Evan Runner, who was neither Dutch nor Christian Reformed. He had first tasted the heady wine of Dooyeweerdianism while a student at Westminster Seminary, and then continued his studies at the Free University in Amsterdam. He arrived in Grand Rapids to teach philosophy at Calvin College in 1951. Henry Stob, a long-time professor in the department, describes their first meeting: "To welcome him to the college, and to lay out to him what courses we would like him to teach, I visited him at his home in midsummer and was treated to a lengthy discourse on what constitutes a truly Calvinistic philosophy and how he, a junior fresh out of graduate school, was disposed to articulate it."[22] Departmental attitudes did not seem to thaw much in the next decade. Runner and Nicholas Wolterstorff traded prickly exchanges about Runner's lectures, "The Relation of the Bible to Learning."[23]

But Runner was lionized by others. The editors of *Torch and Trumpet* welcomed his "courageous" speech (originally delivered, of course, in Dutch as "Het Roer Om"), in which Runner argued

[20] Church newsletter, *Onward*, July, 1958, 9; the article was reprinted in *Church and Nation*, July 22, 1958.

[21] Calvin Seerveld, "Perspective for Our Christian Colleges," *Christianity Today*, September 13, 1963, 10.

[22] Henry Stob, *Summoning Up Remembrance* (Grand Rapids: Eerdmans, 1995), 312.

[23] *Reformed Journal*, December, 1960, 15-24.

passionately for separate Christian organizations.[24] In subsequent issues of the magazine, Runner reiterated his slogans and assailed established CRC worthies such as Leonard Verduin, William Spoelhof, Henry Stob, and Dirk Jellema. Runner also became the guru for the Groen Club, composed of (mostly Canadian) Calvin students who espoused the AACS views.

Besides academic and ideological issues, the Calvin College administration also had to deal with the matter of meager financial support from the Canadian CRC and the potential loss of Canadian students. One solution was sought in the appointment of a part-time field agent to represent Calvin's cause. The Reverend George Hoytema, a retired pastor, served in this position for some time. His reports to the administration make for interesting reading, as he tries to chart his way through the (often legitimate) claims and complaints of the Canadian constituency and the perspective of the college. In addition, Calvin and the AACS conducted a series of meetings, attempting to improve relations. These efforts were successful, for the relationship between Calvin and the Canadian branch of the CRC, including the AACS, began to improve measurably. A dialogue between Nicholas Wolterstorff of Calvin and Hendrik Hart of the ICS also helped assuage the conflict. Wolterstorff presented a history and analysis of the tensions, setting forth both merits and demerits of the AACS. Hart responded with a gracious "open letter" (including an apology of sorts) and assured his readers that the AACS would be much less polemical than it had been in the past.[25] Further signs of good will came later, when Calvin and the ICS began to sponsor conferences together and to exchange faculty occasionally. Today the rapport between the two institutions is cordial.

Even though the relationship between the AACS and Calvin College was at times acrimonious (and the accusations from the AACS often excessive and unfair), the overall outcome was beneficial

24 H. Evan Runner, "Het Roer Om," *Torch and Trumpet,* April, 1953, 1-4.
25 See *Reformed Journal,* December 1974, pp. 9-16 and March 1975, pp. 25-28.

in several ways. First, the clamor of the AACS made Calvin more aware of the Canadian branch of the CRC. Calvin learned that this branch had unique educational needs; this awareness gave rise, in due time, to the teaching of Canadian history and Canadian literature at the college. More importantly, Calvin was reminded of the riches of its continental Reformed tradition. Even though Calvin College and Seminary had always retained their theological heritage, they had also absorbed (at times uncritically) much of their North American milieu. For example, the defense of capitalism, expressions of superpatriotism, infiltration of fundamentalism, acceptance of secular tendencies in American universities—these were present in both church and school. To have these views challenged (noisily!) by recent arrivals from the Netherlands was a valuable wake-up call. The AACS challenge prompted Calvin to renew its deliberation about the Christian calling in scholarship, especially in the integration of faith and learning.[26]

Summing Up

How does one evaluate these voices of censure? The history of both the CRC and of Calvin College is rich and multifaceted, filled

[26]A note about names and terminology: The original name of the AACS was ARSS—Association for Reformed Scientific Studies. (One wag noted that one could tell that the proponents were not truly a part of North America yet, since they did not seem to catch the import of their inelegant acronym.) The chief architects of the philosophy promoted by the AACS were Herman Dooyeweerd and D.H.Th. Vollenhoven, both professors at the Free Universityof Amsterdam. The shorthand "Dooyeweerdianism" for the movement acknowledges the debt to Dooyeweerd. (Never, as far as I know, "Vollenhovenism"). Another shorthand was "WdW." WdW is an acronym for *Wijsbegeerte der Wetsidee,* both the title for Dooyeweerd's most famous work and the designation of his philosophy. At other times *wetsidee* was rendered as "cosmonomic" and the philosophy identified as such. The designation, "Toronto Movement," points to the location of the Institute for Christian Studies in Toronto. Since a well-known series of annual lectures was held in Unionville (Ontario), the movement was sometimes identified with that location, and their opponents sometimes called adherents "Unionvillains."

A fine, informal look at this period and some of the dynamics is provided in three brief articles by Ralph Koops, "25 Years in Canada," in *The Banner,* Feb. 21, Feb. 28, March 14, 1975.

with subtleties and nuances. The discussion above does not catch all this complexity, but it does show some of the reasons for conflict between church and school. I have also sought to demonstrate the array of the conflicts as well as the spirit in which they were conducted. For example, the denunciation by the ACRL was generally vituperative, whereas the critique of the AACS was ultimately constructive.

It is also well to remember that the criticism of Calvin College was often voiced by those who were basically loyal to the school, although they disagreed with some particular emphasis or decision or speaker. Their disagreement was expressed in moderate tone, against the background of approval and support. And let me restate a previous theme: for most of its history Calvin College received overwhelming approval and support from the CRC, and both church and college were enriched by their close association. This qualification is not provided to minimize the import of the more aggressive criticism, but to retain a sense of perspective.

6

Keeping an Eye on the Students

Relations between college students and their neighbors or constituents often have been rocky. In 1354 the students at Oxford, England, so angered the townspeople that they retaliated:

> A mob assembled, armed with bows and arrows and other weapons; they attacked every scholar who passed, and even fired at the Chancellor when he attempted to allay the tumult. The justly indignant Chancellor retorted by ringing St Mary's bell and a mob of students assembled, also armed. A battle royal raged till nightfall, at which time the fray ceased, "no one scholar or townsman being killed or mortally wounded or maimed."[1]

The annals of Calvin College relate no such mêlée, and overall, Calvin's students have been responsible citizens. However, students did often exasperate their neighbors and supporters. In this account I will deal not so much with the common complaints about college students, such as loud parties or parking on neighbors' lawns. I will

1 Alexander De Conde, *Student Activism: Town and Gown in Historical Perspective* (New York, Scribner, 1971), 34.

focus on those issues that arose out of Calvin's relationship with the CRC.

Keeping the Sabbath Holy

The correspondence files of various Calvin presidents, especially of president Spoelhof, frequently address the observance (or rather, the nonobservance) of the Sabbath. To understand the controversy about Sundays, one must realize the importance of proper Sunday observance in the CRC. The "Index to Synodical Decisions" is sometimes a good barometer of CRC issues. Under "Sunday Labor" from 1857-1880, one finds the following topics: Brewery work and milk delivery on the Sabbath; apiary work on the Sabbath; instruction in Holland language in the Sunday schools on the Sabbath. Later years added questions about Sunday work in greenhouses and gas manufacturing establishments, as well as defense factory labor in time of war.

In all these cases the judgment required from synod concerned the question: May this work be performed as either a work of *mercy* or of *necessity*? Some synods ruled certain tasks appropriate (such as milking cows); at other times it was not sure if the particular task was essential (such as brewery and apiary work). (Of course, a Baptist church of the time would have judged the brewery labor not on the basis of Sunday work but on the production of beer.) Until the 1960s, the church was generally able to retain its policy of no work on Sundays, but after that time one finds increasing laxity in enforcing the standard.

Related to Sunday work was Sunday shopping. Christian Reformed members did not operate their shops and stores or go shopping. They also opposed any stores remaining open on Sundays, since such selling and buying desecrated the Sabbath. It was therefore the church's responsibility to keep stores and store owners in line. In Grand Rapids, for example, the popular Meijer department stores were boycotted by many CRC people when Meijer announced Sunday hours in 1969. In Ontario, Canada, the CRC was in the forefront of those protesting a change in Canada's anti-Sunday shopping laws.

Apart from "work," there were other ways of transgressing the Sabbath. C. Huissen, a prominent pastor, summed up: "Sabbath desecration can take many forms. It is agreed that a man who paints his house on Sunday, packs a picnic basket, patronizes commercial sports or amusements...is guilty of this sin."[2] Driving an automobile was to be limited to going to church or performing works of mercy. Moreover, the Sunday newspaper was considered "the greatest single instrument of unholy Sabbath desecration today."[3]

Thus it is obvious that "Sunday observance" was a crucial aspect of CRC identity. *Banner* editor Andrew Kuyvenhoven put it more strongly: "Until about twenty-five years ago our strict observance of the Lord's Day as a day of rest and worship was the most outstanding trait in the lifestyle of Christian Reformed people." [4]

Just as increasing disregard of traditional Sunday observance caused dissension and censure in local congregations, so it caused questions about Sunday practices at Calvin College—although Calvin always was very "conservative" in its Sunday policies. Even in the 1990s, no academic or recreational events or organized sports were sponsored on Sundays, and the library remained firmly locked. Still, the constituency was uneasy at times. The most frequent complaint was the need for Sunday travel at the end of vacations. Since classes often resumed on Monday mornings, students were "forced" to travel back to Grand Rapids on Sunday. In one letter, thirty parents from Denver expressed their concern to the board of trustees. President Spoelhof's response explained in great detail the problems with planning an academic calendar and how the administration tried valiantly to avoid such problems. But "if the

2 "Sunday Entertainment," *Torch and Trumpet*, Feb. 1962, p. 4.

3 J.M. Vande Kieft, "The Sunday Newspaper," *The Banner*, Aug. 8, 1941,728.

4 *The Banner*, Sept. 26, 1983, 7. (This issue of *The Banner* devotes several articles to the Sabbath-Sunday issue. Predictably, even the mildest suggestion that the traditional observance may have been neither biblical nor Reformed elicited stalwart opposition in subsequent letters to the editor.)

students cannot get back without Sunday travel, their parents should see to it that they get back by the Saturday following Thanksgiving."[5]

Even the hours close to Sunday were problematic to some. The college had always avoided Saturday evening sports but in 1966 began to schedule some Saturday evening basketball games. That appeared perilously close to Sunday, and the First Christian Reformed Church of Cutlerville expressed concern. The president explained that such games would not be scheduled with distant colleges, and that all the Saturday events would end by ten o'clock.[6]

Sports were not the only danger zone. The 1963 fall music programs of the college had been submitted to the *Grand Rapids Press*, and the listing appeared in the Sunday edition. President Spoelhof allowed that this was unfortunate, but mentioned the mitigating circumstance that the Sunday *Press* was printed on Saturday and available on newsstands by 8:00 p.m.[7]

By the year 2000, the Sunday paper was no longer looked upon as unholy Sabbath desecration, and Sunday observance in both church and college had been relaxed considerably. Still, the campus remains very quiet on Sundays. Even sacred music performances are scheduled after the evening services in local churches, thus keeping the Sabbath in (old-fashioned) CRC style.

The other feature of Sunday observance concerned worship services and student attendance at those services. When church and school were relatively small, the supervision of the student's spiritual life was shared by the home congregation and college staff and faculty. By 1949 (when enrollment had increased to about 1,400 students), such informal supervision seemed no longer possible, because Classis Grand Rapids East reported "certain alarming conditions among the students at Calvin College." The classis

[5] William Spoelhof Correspondence, March 15, 1960. The Spoelhof correspondence is housed in the Calvin Heritage Hall Archives.

[6] Spoelhof Correspondence, May 23, 1966.

[7] Spoelhof Correspondence, January 13, 1964.

recommended that all CRC students away from home be required to join a Grand Rapids congregation as a condition of enrollment (*Acts of Synod*, 1949, 410, 411). Synod found this requirement too extreme and ruled instead that students "are expected to transfer their membership to a local church of their choice" (*Acts*, 1949, 60). Both classis and synod wished to encourage (and supervise) student church attendance and "to guard the sanctity of the Holy Sacraments." The latter phrase was a reference to the CRC practice of "close(d) Communion," in which only members of a local congregation could participate in the Lord's Supper, with others being allowed to do so only with the express permission of the local consistory.

Church membership continued to be an important question—partly because some students became lax about their worship attendance and there seemed to be no effective way of monitoring and controlling such laxity. In 1953 the college and synod agreed on an arrangement of students obtaining temporary student membership in Grand Rapids churches. An elaborate system of record keeping included a "Student Certificate," an "Acknowledgement" to the home church, and a "School Record Tab" for the college. A separate certificate was made available to students who were not yet professing members, specifying that the student was to attend catechism classes in a Grand Rapids church (*Acts*, 1953, 149-152). Many local congregations took their responsibilities seriously and provided hospitality and spiritual nurture for the students.

Much as one may admire the concern and diligence of church and school to keep tabs on the worship and catechism attendance of the students, most of the students were much less concerned about ecclesiastical machinery and chose to attend (or not attend) whatever churches struck their fancy. Often they made the rounds of churches in which the pulpit was occupied by a popular preacher. When the college moved to the Knollcrest campus, with no churches within walking distance, a new plan was inaugurated—

campus worship services. However, since the Church Order did not permit a "College Church," four local consistories were invited to supervise the "preaching of the Word, administration of sacraments, the liturgy, offerings, operational expense, etc." (*Acts*, 1966, 46-47). This arrangement lasted (with both morning and evening services, in true CRC style) until 1995. At that time the regular Knollcrest worship services, under the supervision of local churches, were discontinued. Students were again urged to attend local morning services (now allowing "both Christian Reformed and others"), and the college initiated an evening LOFT (Living Our Faith Together) service—a service of "worship, discipleship, and fellowship" (*Acts*, 1996, 365-366). By 2000 the LOFT services, with a strong emphasis on "contemporary" worship, were still well attended.

The CRC has always had a vigorous tradition of strict observance of the Lord's Day, with carefully circumscribed lists of (non-) allowable activities. In some families and congregations this observance degenerated into legalistic quibbling: "You may play catch in the backyard, but not in the frontyard; you may not begin traveling until after midnight on Sunday." Church attendance at both morning and evening services also has been a strong tradition, with "oncers" usually not considered to be fit candidates for the office of elder or deacon. These traditions also played a prominent role in Our School, as the church sought to uphold the same practices in the life of Calvin College.

Worldly Amusements

Few issues between church and college lingered as long or were debated as hotly as the question of "worldly amusements." Already in 1925 the board of trustees signaled the danger of worldliness and singled out "theater attendance, dancing, and card-playing" as forbidden practices (Minutes, June 4, 1925, art. 12). Bernard Pekelder summarized the board's stance as follows:

> This early Board action, taken three years prior to the church's official resolutions on worldliness, reflected the mind and spirit of the church at large. It also indicated attitudes which marked the approach of the Board to this problem through succeeding years. First, worldliness was identified very closely with three social activities: movies, dancing, and card-playing. Second, a blanket indictment was laid against all three. Third, the Board officially decided that suspension and expulsion were instruments to be used on students to enforce the ban. Fourth, the Board gave the faculty the responsibility to issue warnings and administer discipline. And it is the last-mentioned that became the crux of the issue, and marked the beginning of an almost unending tension between Board and faculty.[8]

I will deal primarily with the controversy over students attending movies in the local theaters. In the area of amusements, this issue provoked the longest controversy, and it exhibited most clearly the intertwining of church and school. But since the movies were usually lumped together with card playing and dancing under the worldly amusements rubric, I will also touch on those.

In response to several requests, synod 1926 appointed a committee to study the issue of worldly amusements, specifying theater/movie attendance, card playing, and dancing. This committee reported in 1928, and its "Report of the Committee on Worldly Amusements" (*Agenda to Synod*, 4-56) was approved by synod. The report described worldliness and the increasing infiltration of worldliness into the church and specified how the church ought to conduct itself over against the world—not by isolation but by spiritual separation. Synod did recognize the biblical principle of Christian liberty but used a very narrow definition, and involvement in these amusements did not fall in the domain of Christian liberty. Although it was made clear that the trio of amusements were not the sole forbidden area

8 Pekelder, "Role of the Board," 90-91.

of worldliness, the prohibition was focused here. Those church members who did engage in the prohibited amusements and did not repent and desist (for example, from "dancing at a public dance-hall of evil repute" (p. 50) should be disciplined and eventually excommunicated (50-56).

After 1928 the church tried to digest the report. Most members of the denomination agreed with the intent of synod, certainly its staunch attempt to preserve the church from the evil influence of the world. Many articles in *The Banner* reinforced the sense of alarm about worldliness. Editor H.J. Kuiper, especially, did not tire of warning his readers. In one article, significantly titled "Sodom and Gomorrah," he argued that even this designation would be too mild for Hollywood, with its "vile products of the most pernicious commercialized amusement of our day....The movie-theater is the open sewer in the city of Amusement from which men and women of perverted tastes seek to satisfy their thirst for pleasure."[9] However, others in the church found the official stance too extreme. Card playing, especially, was considered an innocuous pastime, and synod was enlisted to define card playing! Synod tried, but after a three-fold "*Whereas...,*" produced no more than a reference to synod 1928 (*Acts*, 1932, 38).

Moreover, movie attendance and even dance were on the increase, and in 1951 synod was asked to clarify both the prohibitions and the church's treatment of those who strayed off the path. The 1951 report (*Acts*, 126-169) largely confirmed the stringency of 1928. To no avail. Especially with the infiltration of television into CRC homes (sometimes with the antenna hidden in the attic) the church caved in to the movie onslaught. After all, who could object to *I Love Lucy* and *The Sound of Music*? By 1966 the official posture had changed radically. The report of that year acknowledged that many CRC members were regular television and movie watchers, that many films were worthwhile, and that Christians ought to be involved in trying to transform the theater, rather than avoiding it.

9 H.J. Kuiper, "Sodom and Gomorrah," *The Banner,* December 12, 1947, 1380.

The title of the report is telling: instead of the "sewer in the city of Amusement," the focus now is on "the Film Arts and the Church" (*Acts*, 1966, 316-361).[10]

Given the general condemnation of movies in the denomination, it is no wonder that Calvin College would become the flashpoint for the controversy. The young people of the church would be the most tempted to attend movies, especially young people no longer under the direct supervision of their parents. As indicated above, the board's prohibition in 1925 preceded the denomination's policy by three years, and the board continued to uphold its ban rigorously—partly because of its conviction, partly because it saw itself as representing the CRC.

Even though many faculty and students agreed with the denomination's warnings against worldliness and against the harmful influence of many movies, they were less keen on the board's absolute stance. The frequent complaints lodged against the students' attendance at movies is a clear indication that they flouted the rules. The faculty, moreover, resisted their role as enforcers. Many faculty found the prohibition too stringent, and they found the policing of students both distasteful and unsuccessful. Already in 1932 then president R.B. Kuiper reflected the frustration of both faculty and students. "Our attempts to enforce the rule of the Board prohibiting theater and movie attendance, dancing, and card playing have met with the usual difficulties. The rule is very unpopular with the majority of our students and, unless one should institute a detective bureau, is impossible of fool-proof enforcement." He asked the board to *define* the three offenses, and "may we know whether the Board intends that transgressors of this rule shall be disciplined as are those who break a recognized moral law?"[11] In 1937 the issue

10 A fine article detailing the history of this CRC issue is William Romanowski, "John Calvin Meets The Creature from the Black Lagoon: The Christian Reformed Church and the Movies 1928-1966, *Christian Scholar's Review*, 25, 1, (1995), 47-62. My only point of disagreement with Romanowski is his characterization of the 1951 report. Romanowski finds that "this report made movie attendance a matter of individual conscience." I interpret the report as essentially a reiteration of 1928.

11 "Report of the College President 1932," 9.

came to a head, initially because of the transgression of one student. She attended movies, freely admitted she did, and refused to desist. The board came down heavily. Its executive committee decided to suspend the student for four weeks and to deny her financial aid and the opportunity to go on a spring choir tour. The faculty was not pleased. They requested a special meeting with the committee. The record of the minutes (below) is rather lengthy but makes for instructive reading; it clearly shows the importance of the question in the denomination, the spectrum of opinions and practices, and the untenable policing duty of the faculty. (We have such a complete summary because of the diligence of the committee's secretary, L.J. Lamberts.)

Board Executive Committee

Meeting held Monday Feb. 15, 1937

1. The chairman called this special meeting to order at 1:45 P.M.

2. A committee of the college faculty composed of President R. Stob, Professors J. Broene, J. Vanden Bosch, P. J. Hoekstra, and H. J. Ryskamp. The last named served as the spokesman of the committee. The faculty felt that they should talk with the Ex. Committee about the case of discipline concerning which the committee had given instructions. The young lady in question had been frank with Miss Timmer about her attendance of the movie, while there are others who do attend but lie when they are questioned as to this matter. When fac. faced the question what to do about this case, it considered that there was a breaking of a rule, but at the same time that this was the first case, and that the psychological effect upon the student had to be considered. Now it so happens that the committee's penalty is far more drastic than that imposed by the faculty. Prof. J. Broene added that the reason why the faculty requested this meeting was because the majority of its

members did not feel ready to accede to this request, and he expressed the hope that since the relations had ever been ideal that this matter would not lead to difficulties. Prof. Hoekstra asked how faculty would have to go about in enforcing this rule, seeing that from the nature of the case the penalty would fall upon the honest students. There are already hard feelings between the faculty on the one hand and the parents and friends of the young lady, as many as 177 students have signed a petition asking for her reinstatement, and a petition from the Glee club that the 3d point shall not be enforced.

Prof. Vanden Bosch ventured to give the information that it is no open secret that consistories fail to take action in this matter, but that the faculty is called upon to put on the screws. He said he found that young people are attending movies not merely in Grand Rapids and vicinity but in all parts of our church.

Prof. J. Broene stated that the difficulty was not with the outsiders but with those of our own church and that the question remained how to approach this matter so that the dishonest ones would get away with their movie attendance and the honest ones be penalized. A rule and a law can be enforced only if public opinion is back of it. This became evident when the 18th amendment was written in the Constitution.

Hoekstra said it was unfortunate that Calvin College is regarded as a hellhole where students attend movies, while at other places they do not attend. Cicero's minister claimed that their boys and girls did not attend while Mr. A. S. De Jong claims that in Chicago some of the children of the grades will even skip school to attend the movies. In Dr. Hoekstra's opinion the church has already lost its fight in this matter.

Vanden Bosch asked to what extent the rule must be enforced with card playing, whether this applies to Rook, flinch, etc. He added that Wheaton can maintain a distinctive atmosphere because the students form it. But at Calvin it is different. Parents have no objections to their children's attending the movies, and in such cases it is hard for Calvin to apply the rule. In other cases there are parents who suppose their children do not go to the movies while they are attending regularly.

Prof. Hoekstra added that he can point to elders in our church who do not care about the rule at all, but laugh at it.

Prof. Broene stated that...the faculty sees the possibility that the Board will make matters more difficult and demand that screws be applied more tightly, but what would faculty have to do in case 100 students should come and say they had gone also. He stated that there was no desire to rebel against the Board nor did it mean that there should be no rule....

Dr. Hoekstra stated that if the faculty is going to handle all the cases that are brought to the attention of Miss Timmer and of Dr. Meeter the position of these two people becomes untenable. It will look as if they are betraying the confidence of the students. He added that in his opinion the church within 15 or 20 years is going to recapitulate on this point; he pointed out that he was not sympathetic to the movie at all, seeing that his interests were in another line.

Prof. Broene declared that it would be a bad sign if the faculty would allow students to attend the theater indiscriminately. If we fail in this matter, it is going to hurt us in the end. He added that he had advocated that a committee of the faculty would talk this matter over with the Board.

When the secretary asked whether the faculty had made a decision as to the penalty, he received an affirmative reply.

> He stated he did not know there was such a decision, for if there was, why should the Executive Committee make a ruling as to this matter? Dr. Stob answered that he had mentioned that a decision had been taken.
>
> 3. After the committee had left, it was decided to state the following:
>
> a. That it was not clear to all the members of the Executive Committee at the February 1st meeting that the faculty had already taken a definite decision;
>
> b. That the Executive Committee, while laboring under the impression that the faculty wanted its opinion on this matter, it acted accordingly and asked the faculty to take the following steps with respect to the young woman in question:
>
> 1. To suspend her for four weeks;
>
> 2. To disqualify her from receiving further assistance from the N. Y. A. funds; and
>
> 3. To prevent her from going with the Glee Club on its tour to the east this spring.
>
> c. That the Executive Committee is still of the opinion that the stipulated penalty should be applied, but that if it appears that it will be impossible for the young woman to graduate in June if the four-week period is enforced, the committee advises the faculty to reduce this to a period of two weeks.

This meeting was not the end. The executive committee, hoping for a stronger faculty stance, requested the faculty to draw up a unified statement. The faculty, however, differed substantially among themselves, and they were not able to produce a united front.[12] Now the board was displeased. It considered the lack of unanimity "nothing less than tragic." They continued with an appeal to the school as a denominational institution: "Our school

12 "Report of the President, 1937."

is a church school and it is the 'West Point' of our denomination, the training camp for those who are to be our leaders. The faculty should unitedly hold high the moral ideals for which our church officially stands" (BOT Minutes, 1937, Art. 110, 113). There is no record of the faculty's reaction to this scolding, but one can well imagine their chagrin at this dressing down. The board had also discussed the possibility to "call in the whole Faculty," for further confrontation. It was probably well that they stopped at sending each professor a copy of the resolutions. But the impasse was not resolved.

The battle was joined once again in 1940, when the Committee of Ten (see chapter 3) made its report and recommendations. "Worldly Amusements" were high on their agenda and they affirmed the previous stance of the board. The committee and the board affirmed the rule that continued movie attendance should be punished by expulsion (BOT Minutes, 1940, Art. 64). Synod of that same year also reaffirmed that stance (*Acts*, 98) and wondered about the possibility of showing "pictures of a high order" on campus.

After 1950 the issue of students attending movies became muted. No doubt the increasing acceptance of movie attendance in the CRC, coupled with the popularity of television, made the prohibition untenable. The 1962-1963 *Student Handbook* was the first not to print the prohibition against the three worldly amusements. After this time the arena shifted to films shown on campus.

I will not trace the controversies of films on campus in detail. The dynamics of the disagreement were often similar to those of students attending the movies: the content of the films was in violation of the moral stance of the CRC; Calvin College was a CRC institution, and therefore showing the films on campus was wrong. Although hundreds of films were shown that elicited no comment from the constituency, approximately fifteen films caused considerable controversy. These included *Bonnie and Clyde, Chinatown, La Dolce Vita, Oh, God!, Play It Again, Sam, Saturday Night Fever, Taxi Driver,* and *The Deer Hunter.*

The board and the president's office received a flood of letters protesting these films. One missive is indicative of the motivation and spirit of many letter writers. Scrawled on the back of a Calvin College "Pledge Reminder" a disgruntled (former) donor wrote: "I am returning your reminder. The last straw was placed on the camel's back when you upheld the devil's act of a mere man impersonating our God in the showing of *Oh, God!* I only wish there was some way to stop our quotas to make Calvin straighten out!"

I will discuss the controversy surrounding two films, both because these were the most stormy and because they clearly display the issues that were at stake.

On December 8, 1973, a Christian Reformed couple wandered into Calvin's Fine Arts Center to see the film *Cabaret,* which had been advertised in the *Grand Rapids Press.* Their description of the film, sent in a letter to all CRC consistories, left no doubt about their evaluation. "The story in this film was filthy; the language was dirty, swearing, and blasphemous; it showed pre-marital sex, drunkenness, homosexuality, and abortion as if it was an everyday way of life....To say the least, we were very much disturbed by what we saw.... If we say nothing, we become a part of the working of the devil, having seen it with our own eyes....We URGE you, as a consistory, to take action against this ungodly activity at Calvin College before it is too late! You are holding the key! Will our Calvin College once again become a 'Christian' College, or is it lost? The decision is YOURS!"[13]

The couple had a two-hour conversation with President Spoelhof and then sent off the letter. Over a hundred alarmed churches corresponded with the college administration and BOT, who in turn responded to each letter received. The college responses generally explained that a film may portray evil without condoning the evil, that a Christian might be able to view such a film and learn

[13] Spoelhof Correspondence, 1974. In this chapter and in chapter 7 I will not cite the names of those who corresponded with the presidents and other Calvin College officials.

from it, and that the purpose of showing films at Calvin is as much for education as entertainment.[14]

A subsequent controversial movie was *A Clockwork Orange*, a 1971 film by the famous director Stanley Kubrick—a film often criticized for its depiction of sex and violence. It was scheduled to be shown January 8, 1977, with an introduction by Nicholas Wolterstorff, professor of philosophy. *A Clockwork Orange* was pulled from the schedule by President Diekema on December 30, 1976—barely half a year into his presidency. Behind the proposed showing and the cancellation of the movie was a complex history, as well as many voices and forces, both on and off campus. Certainly the contested place of movies and movie attendance in the CRC was a major factor. There was no unanimity in the denomination about movies as either art or entertainment, and there was even less agreement on the propriety of watching or showing particular films. In addition, the college, especially through its Film Arts Committee (FAC), considered the showing of films an educational function, with the films to be followed by discussion and evaluation. The constituency, on the other hand, viewed films primarily as entertainment and judged many titles to be reprehensible choices. Thus church and school were at great odds. (One telling example of the great divide between the college and its constituency is a brief sentence in the minutes of the FAC: "The Film Arts Committee is aware, of course, that some viewers will find the film disturbing and may in turn complain about its showing."[15] The FAC seemed far removed from the real feelings "out there".)

It is also important to keep in mind that the controversy divided the campus as well. Many students and faculty protested the showing of particular films, either before or after the showing. For example, in the fall of 1976 six hundred students expressed their concern by signing a petition requesting a review of the selection

[14] Spoelhof Correspondence, 1974.
[15] Diekema Papers, Box 203.

policy of the FAC, since many of the films chosen were totally inappropriate for a Christian college.[16]

There are perhaps few issues in the world of American Christian higher education that produced such prolonged and intense controversy between a college and its sponsoring denomination as the movie controversy did at Calvin College. How does one account for this intensity?

Part of the reason can be found in the earlier history of the Christian church. Drama and theater have been suspect in many eras of church history. The most frequent objections to the theater were the content of the plays and the licentiousness often associated with the theater world. Plays often portrayed immoral characters performing wicked deeds, and the virtuous life was frequently mocked. The people performing in the theater were usually regarded as no better than the characters they portrayed, and theater attendees were also considered disreputable. This appraisal of the theater, shared by both continental and English Calvinistic churches, was certainly part of the CRC heritage. Some church authorities went beyond this denunciation and considered all acting wrong. No less an authority than Abraham Kuyper judged that acting was living a lie. "This systematic living in untruth is, according to our conviction, harmful to a person's Christian life, and therefore not permitted for the Christian."[17] This view was not officially adopted by the CRC but was certainly held by many.

The condemnation of the theater was usually transferred to the "moving pictures" by many churches, and in the 1920s one finds fundamentalist groups issuing denunciations similar to the CRC statement of 1928. However, many denominations moderated their stance; they advocated discretion in attending movies and published reviews and lists of approved and non-approved movies.

As noted above, the CRC continued its nonnegotiable stance into the 1960s. One factor that contributed to this radical position was

16 *Chimes*, Jan. 14, 1977, 4.
17 Abraham Kuyper, *Publiek Vermaak* (Amsterdam, Drukkerij de Standaard, 1880), 42.

the Reformed doctrine of the antithesis. Those who maintain that there is an absolute distinction between the kingdom of God and the kingdom of darkness will tend to detect absolutes of good and evil in their environment and culture. In the case of the CRC, the problem of Americanization and assimilation also played a role. One way to preserve the purity of the church was to ward off as much as possible "American" influences in the life of the church and CRC families.

Calvin College became the battle ground for this controversy, because "our school" was seen as an extension of the CRC. But here we see one area where the college began to break out of its denominational confines. Whereas most theologians in the CRC stressed the antithesis in doctrine and life, the college often emphasized the doctrine of common grace, especially in the approach to culture and learning. If one could learn from Plato's *The Republic*, the college argued, then perhaps also from Sophocles's *Oedipus Rex*. And from *Oedipus Rex*, it was only a few short steps to *On the Waterfront* and then to *A Clockwork Orange*.

Finally, the increasing polarization in the CRC between conservatives and progressives also played a significant role. Most of the criticism about movies at Calvin College came from the conservative wing of the denomination. The showing of immoral movies was seen by conservatives as a manifestation of the decay of the CRC. The college thus became a target partly because it allowed the conservatives to vent their frustration and anger about the denomination.

As with other disputes between school and church, the one about movie attendance and films shown on campus caused both misunderstanding and distress. Those protesting the movies were genuinely concerned about the encroachment of secularism and about the pernicious influence of a non-Christian culture. Those defending Calvin College and its policies stressed the importance of Christian involvement in and shaping of culture, especially in the arena of Christian higher education. Through it all, Calvin College again had to define its mission and determine its relationship to the CRC.

Student Publications

In his history of Calvin College, John Timmerman offers a careful and wise discussion of various student publications at Calvin College.[18] He especially deals at some length with the student newspaper, *Chimes*. Lauding the many brilliant editors and writers, lamenting the frequent rhetorical excesses, Timmerman concludes that he agrees with the school's ideals that school publications "must reflect a living and thoughtful Reformed perspective on life," but he adds, "I would immediately rule out censorship as a way to achieve them."[19] Given the tension between objectionable writing and the rejection of censorship, the question in Calvin's history then became: How best to deal with controversial student writing?

There had been some critique of student writings since the beginning of the college, but the criticism began to gather force in the 1950s. For example, an editorial in the March 14, 1952, *Chimes* (a rather inept stereotype of preseminary students) provoked a pastor to demand "an apology . . . for this scurrilous attack."[20] A few years later, the winter 1956 *Literary Review* contained a poignant short story of a prostitute. Certainly in the year 2000 the story would hardly rate a constituency frown, but in the mid-fifties the story was considered highly objectionable. The publication committee withdrew the issue from circulation after it had been distributed on campus, but copies had reached some parents. A minister wrote a letter of concern to President Spoelhof: "The *Review* has been circulated rapidly, with a growing undercurrent of dissatisfaction. . . . This has done much to sour our people on Calvin College."[21]

[18] Timmerman, *Promises*, 176-83.
[19] Ibid., 181.
[20] Spoelhof Correspondence, 1952.

The furor over student publications assumed gale force in the 1960s and 1970s. Much of the offence was created by the annual spoof issues produced by the *Chimes* staff.[22] When the 1967 spoof issue, *Bong,* appeared, reactions came forth promptly and angrily. A long letter to President Spoelhof summed up the contents,

> its many disrespectful allusions to yourself, Scripture, John Calvin, hymnology and conservative ideology, much of which borders on the blasphemous. Its left wing slant and generally contumacious attitude go far beyond the merely humorous....Again, the question is, what are we going to do about it?....Appeasement and compromise will get us nowhere. The offending students and their faculty mentors to the extent responsible must be gotten rid of....Trusting that God will grant you the holy boldness and Elijah-like zeal to drive out the heathen from the Lord's inheritance.[23]

Anyone acquainted with the history of Calvin College will have heard about the (in)famous *Bananer.* Produced by the *Chimes* staff as the spring 1970 spoof issue, it reverberated long and far in church and college.[24] *Bananer* was a sixteen-page parody of the denominational weekly, *The Banner.* Every page and column, every author and contributor, every illustration and stylistic trait was parodied and satirized to perfection. The young people's column was represented by "Jongen Folks and Their Dominees," featuring Tobias Pekker, dominee of the Overdiesel Philistine Rewarmed Crutch, and Stanley Prune, a freshman at Warp College and pathfinder in the Galvanized Kadeters." An obituary read, "CHUCKLESON, Siebs, age 21; May 15, 1970. Died of heart attack while in crucial confrontation with Rev. John Vander Phlegm

21 Spoelhof Correspondence, 1956.

22 For an extensive oveview of the *Chimes* in the 1960s, see David Larson, "Evangelical Christian Higher Education, Culture, and Social Conflict," Ph.D. dissertation, Loyola University of Chicago, 1992.

23 Spoelhof Correspondence, 1967.

24 See Timmerman, *Promises,* 180-81, for his perspective. See *The Banner,* April 24, 1995, for a retrospect, "Bananer Perpetrators Confess 25 Years Later."

and the entire PRC synod. Mother, Winfred, father, Herman Hubers, 16 brothers, 1 sister." And so it continued with enough cleverness to amuse some in college and church and enough impudence and rudeness to offend many of the rest.

The major salvo of horrified reproof came from the editor of the real *Banner*, the Reverend John Vander Ploeg, who wrote a four-page editorial, "Do We Just Laugh This Off?" His opening and closing paragraphs show the tenor of his article:

> *Chimes*, Calvin College student newspaper, recently had the audacity and the gall to lampoon THE BANNER by publishing a mock issue ("The Bananer") in which the perpetrators of it shamelessly made a mockery of the Christian Reformed Church (calling it throughout "the Philistine Rewarmed Crutch"), our church paper's use of Scripture, morality, Dordt College, as well as other objects of their scorn. The whole thing is deplorable, a disgrace to Calvin College, and at times nothing less than blasphemy.... Finally, let us be truly fervent in prayer for those persons who have given such offense and sinned so grievously.[25]

President Spoelhof responded with "An Open Letter From Dr. William Spoelhof to the Editor," trying to explain the posture of the administration but also rebuking the editor: "Now that you have vented your angry blast, I want you to know that I also regret your action and your words."[26] Spoelhof's reaction to Vander Ploeg's "angry blast" was shared by others, and there were many who thought the *Bananer* both clever and a needed corrective for an out-of-touch denomination. But these folks were vastly outnumbered (at least publicly) by those who took offense. The Association of Christian Reformed Laymen fanned the flames of controversy, both by their editorializing about "the scurrilous *Bananer*," and by reprinting it and distributing it throughout the church. Petitions were circulated in several classes of the denomination, demanding

25 *Banner*, June 19, 1970, 8-11.
26 *Banner*, June 26, 1970, 19.

the expulsion of the guilty students, removal of faculty and board members who had condoned *The Bananer*, and curtailment of financial support for the college.

Soon letters started pouring in, and the administration and the trustees shifted to damage control operation. The board published a resolution expressing "reprimand and regret" (BOT Minutes, May 18, 1970, 31), while the executive committee counted two hundred letters received in protest and discussed the problem at great length (Minutes, August 6, 1970, Art. 9). In a subsequent report Spoelhof admitted, "In my twenty years as President of Calvin College, no one College incident touched off a greater storm than did the production of the student spoof last May. . . . Never has my mail been heavier. I faithfully answered all letters, no matter how vindictive—or complimentary—the tone."[27]

Although the reactions had subsided by the time of this report (February 1971), the publication of *Bananer* continued to be pointed out as a sign of the spiritual corrosion at Calvin College. Why such a violent reaction? First, the publication itself. The publication of satire nearly always follows a predictable path. Those who write satire regard their writing as clever and their targets as deserving and needing exposure by ridicule. Those who read the satire regard their cause (and themselves) as noble, and any attack is seen as an assault on the true, the good, and the beautiful; the humor, moreover, is considered impudent and irreverent. That familiar pattern certainly came true here. The writers saw the CRC (and *The Banner*) as reactionary, narrow, humorless, and devoid of genuine biblical insight. In other words, deserving and needing mockery. The offended constituency saw itself as defending the traditions of both church and country, and the *Bananer* attack as an affront to God and king.

Secondly, the timing of the parody was bound to cause a furor. The country had seen nearly a decade of wrenching division about the Vietnam War and about many social issues, with campuses

[27] "Report of the President," February 1, 1971.

often at odds with a conservative establishment. Although Calvin College demonstrations were mild compared to those at many universities, Calvin had become highly suspect. Moreover, just the year before, many in the CRC had been fuming at Calvin students for their protest march against the CRC churches and Christian schools in Cicero, Illinois, about their refusal to admit black students. Several campus speakers (such as Father Groppi) had aroused strong opposition, worship services of students were criticized, and the counter culture (including long hair on males and short skirts on females) was enough in evidence to shock the constituency. If church-college relations resembled the proverbial tinderbox, then the *Bananer* was the spark that ignited it.

In addition, as we have noted before, the relations between conservatives and progressives in the denomination were becoming more and more strained. Conservative pastors and congregations were beginning to leave the denomination, and the belligerent stance of the Association of Christian Reformed Laymen further encouraged division. The appearance of The *Bananer* became proof to many that the "liberals" in the denomination (who were thought to be concentrated at Calvin) were coming close to destroying the church.

Students as Ambassadors

Judging the Calvin student body and their relation to the CRC by the number of constituency letters in the college archives is hardly accurate. Correspondents will always write more readily to complain and protest than to commend and applaud. That truism certainly applies to constituents' comments about college students. Throughout Calvin's history, one will find compelling evidence that, in spite of frequent criticism, the students were a credit to the college and were appreciated by the denomination. Let me briefly mention some examples of amiable and productive contacts between campus and church.

Near the top of this catalog should be the musical contributions of the college. In Grand Rapids the annual performance of *Messiah* has become a major cultural and religious event, as have the dozens of other music programs offered every season. But the musical events were not limited to Grand Rapids. As early as 1909, the fledgling orchestra performed in Grand Haven and Muskegon. (The church in Zeeland had also extended an invitation, but the consistory cancelled the concert because they held that it was not appropriate for an orchestra to play in church). The Men's Glee Club also traveled to Holland and Muskegon. A report in *The Banner* indicates the favorable reception: "In every way the boys must be encouraged, and [this reporter] sincerely hopes that next year Holland will be prepared to welcome the Club members in a large hall, possibly Carnegie Hall of Hope College."[28] The first extensive tour took place in 1922, when the Glee Club traveled as far as Whitinsville, Massachusetts. Since then the various musical groups have traveled to every corner of the denomination, always to the acclaim of the constituency.[29]

The western Michigan churches and the community at large have benefited greatly from Calvin's many other cultural and educational offerings, in which impressive theater performances rank very high. Calvin students have also been extensively involved in local schools (both public and Christian schools) as student teachers and volunteer tutors. In recent decades many students have volunteered in needy communities. The Spring Vacation work sessions in Appalachia and elsewhere have been especially remarkable.

Of course, appreciation for Calvin students often came after their graduation. A large number of alumni (including many "problem students") have filled professional and church positions in CRC communities. The Christian Schools International network has received thousands of graduates from Calvin, as have CRC pulpits.

Christian Reformed people kept a close eye on Calvin College students. Often they did not appreciate what they saw and they grumbled and complained—sometimes loudly and insistently. More often the churches liked what they saw.

[28] April 30, 1914, 298.

[29] See Seymour Swets, *Fifty Years of Music at Calvin College* (Grand Rapids: Eerdmans, 1973) for many additional details.

7
Watching the Professors

In the early years of Calvin College, the requirements and demands for faculty were rather modest. They were to have the same academic qualifications as professors at other institutions, they were "to possess adequate intellectual capacity…, adequate pedagogical skills…, and not be unqualified for his labor because of old age or weakness" (*Acts of Synod*, 1910, 45). I am confident that all professors who ever taught at Calvin fulfilled those requirements. However, there were many additional expectations that were added over the years, either explicitly or implicitly, and the constituency of the college wanted the faculty to live up to those expectations. If they did not, the professors or the president or the board were put on notice. Here we will survey just two areas in which CRC members found the professors wanting.

Politics

Calvin College professors have always been able to belong to whatever political party they wished and to vote their consciences. However, they were watched closely in expressions of their political views, and not all in the Calvin constituency thought that the faculty should have such freedom. Some statements of disagreement were mild. One student wrote to President Spoelhof, "Even though he is a Democrat, the dean is a fine man."[1] A supporter of the college had stronger reservations: "This letter is written to let you know about our misgivings that there are today teachers in Calvin who are running for office on the Democratic ticket and who are thus publicly professing to be of a mind that teaches the welfare state program and that also embraces the socialistic and paternalistic attitude of the Government. This to me is the absurd thing to behold....It is high time for you as President to speak out."[2]

One of the more spirited debates on political/economic positions took place in 1950. The background for the dispute was a book by the right-wing Roman Catholic author John T. Flynn, *The Road Ahead.* The book militated against communism and socialism and saw American society rush headlong into a socialist abyss. The book was recommended by the National Association of Evangelicals, of which the CRC was a member. Lester De Koster, a recently appointed professor at Calvin, wrote a devastating review of the book and of the NAE's recommendation.[3]

H. J. Kuiper, editor of *The Banner*, responded with vehemence, defending Flynn and assailing De Koster: "Frankly, we can't quite conceive of anyone reacting to Flynn's book without wondering whether he is in sympathy with the socialistic trend in this country." Not content with slurring De Koster, Kuiper further cast doubt on Calvin College: "One thing that worries us is that the men who teach sociology, economics, and related subjects in our College and Christian high schools received their training in these subjects, not at a Calvinistic university, but at the general universities of our land all of which are infected with the Socialistic virus....We wonder just how much attention our Board of Trustees or its Executive

[1] Spoelhof Correspondence D, June 12, 1967.
[2] Spoelhof Correspondence S, October 10, 1964.
[3] Lester De Koster, "Calvin Teacher Protests Against NAE's Commendation of 'The Road Ahead,'" *The Banner*, Aug. 18, 1950, 1020.

Committee, is paying to this danger."[4] The debate between the two men continued in the pages of *The Banner* through November, with very little yielding on either side—no doubt partly because both men relished debate.[5] De Koster received support from eighteeen of his colleagues who protested both Kuiper's argument and his tone.[6] Kuiper responded with heavy sarcasm: "We know our readers share our great respect for the learning and the competence of the men who teach at our College and Seminary; but who is ready to agree with their utterance merely because they are professors at our School and in number eighteen?"[7] Church (as represented by the editor of *The Banner*) and college were obviously far apart.[8]

De Koster was the center of another political controversy ten years later. He and several other Calvin professors spoke in favor of John Kennedy's presidency. In the eyes of many CRC members, this choice for Kennedy was committing a double fault. Not only was the majority of the CRC Republican, but it also harbored strong anti-Catholic fears and feelings. The post-election *Banner* issue carried four items dealing with this issue. One reader summed up the feelings of many: "Prof. De Koster's choice of political affiliation

4 H.J. Kuiper, "Some Observations on Flynn's 'The Road Ahead,'" *Banner*, Aug. 25, 1950, 1028-29

5 James Bratt notes: In De Koster "Kuiper had met more than his match for clever, unforgiving argumentation." *Dutch Calvinism*, 190. See also Bratt's insightful "group-grid" analysis on p. 291, note 7.

6 *The Banner*, Sept. 15, 1950, 1125 and Sept. 29, 1207.

7 "Our Comment on the Report," *The Banner*, Sept. 15, 1125.

8 Interestingly, this public debate was followed a few months later by a rather bizarre appointment process of De Koster. Kuiper had sent a " long communication" to the board, citing many weaknesses of the college and warning against the appointment of De Koster. De Koster was grilled by the board, especially on his views regarding capitalism and the welfare state. He passed the interview, but the board then decided that "we now appoint a committee of two and ask De Koster to accompany them to the *Banner* editor and see if they can confer and agree on a statement agreeable to both whereby to allay the fears which have been aroused in the minds of many of our constituency." The next day, "the DeKoster-Kuiper committee reports having a fine meeting with the brethren. At first the situation appeared ominous, but soon it became obvious they were surprisingly near one another in their views" (BOT Minutes, Feb. 7-11, 1951, Art. 44, 47, 49, 85). In 1952 Kuiper tried to garner support for his suspicions of the college by collecting signatures on a "Petition," but he was able to solicit only 147 names, and synod refused to accept the petition (see Timmerman, *Promises*, 186).

is his business. But it is our business to deny him and his fellow welfare staters the right to use the Commons Building to confuse the minds of our sons and daughters....Our Christian Reformed people do not support Calvin College to give professors opportunity to turn our children against the sound principles of their fathers."[9] Prominent space was also given to an "Open Letter" by a pastor, in which he lamented the harm done to Calvin College because of the political involvement of some professors.[10] This letter was followed by a long response of President Spoelhof, in which he defended the rights of Calvin professors to present unpopular views, but "no professor should use his classroom time to propagandize a partisan point of view."[11] Spoelhof also was able to assure concerned parents that their sons and daughters apparently did remain true to the faith of the fathers: "A student political preference poll was taken just five days before the election, which showed that 90.4% favored Nixon, and 9.6% favored Kennedy." Finally, a missive from De Koster was printed. De Koster expressed that he was sorry that had he been misunderstood, and that he had caused some damage to Calvin. He also expressed his appreciation to Spoelhof for allowing faculty to speak freely, but, "I think it is desirable to refrain from further public discussion within our Reformed and, especially, local community of such views as might in any way be construed as politically partisan."[12] If the letter was intended as an apology, I doubt if very many readers were satisfied by it!

The trustees had also become embroiled in the controversy, and they appointed a Committee on Political Activities of College Professors. The matter was dealt with at length in the February 1961 board meeting. Sydney Youngsma, development secretary, and

[9] John Van Mouwerink, "Objects to Political Activity at Calvin in Recent Campaign," *Banner*, November 18, 1960, 22.

[10] Henry Verduin, "To Lovers of Calvin," *Banner*, November 18, 1960, 11.

[11] "Reply by President Spoelhof," *Banner*, November 18, 1960, 11.

[12] Lester De Koster, "An Open Letter from Prof. De Koster to President of Calvin College," *Banner*, November 18, 1960, 22.

President Spoelhof met with the executive committee of the board. Youngsma reported that in the process of soliciting funds for the college, many supporters had protested vehemently against the professors' political activity. "Phone calls were bitter, even savage, so that at last Mr. Youngsma refused to respond unless people identified themselves....No one can say at this stage how much Calvin will suffer financially. Perhaps the situation can be best analyzed by saying that there is less confidence." Spoelhof reported that he had also been busy putting out fires, and that the faculty had met three times to discuss the matter (Executive Committee Report VI, February 1961).

Professor De Koster was asked to appear before the board, with the outcome that "the Board declare general satisfaction with the interview with Prof. L. De Koster" (BOT Minutes, February 1961, Art. 66). The board also drafted a policy statement on "Political Activities of Professors"; this report was formally adopted in 1962. The statement spells out clearly that faculty are free to affiliate with the political party of their choice, but that they "in accepting a teaching position on the staff of Calvin College and Seminary may be expected to be considerate in exercising their right to freedom of speech and to use caution and discretion..." (BOT Minutes, May 1962, Art. 11).

Fifteen years later another blast at the right wing of American politics elicited strong constituency reaction. The *Reformed Journal* published a "Special Supplement on the Far Right," attacking Barry Goldwater, Carl McIntire, and others in the rightist camp.[13] Since all six authors were Calvin professors, they and the college were branded as socialist sympathizers. Wrote one incensed reader: "Your articles have not only disgusted a large number of good people in our area, but also they smack of some infiltration of Communist leadership into Calvin."[14] Another respondent fumed:

13 Jan. 1965, 11-13.
14 *Reformed Journal*, March, 1965, 22.

"I find this supplement the most revolting, unchristian, Pharisaical, prejudiced and unethical paper I have ever read."[15]

These incidents show clearly that Calvin College professors were watched closely by the CRC constituency. The fact that most members of the CRC were supporters of the Republican Party and were generally on the right of the United States political spectrum made any political departure highly suspect.[16] Several issues were at stake in this conflict. For the faculty, a crucial question was the one of freedom of speech: a professor should have the right to speak and write about political issues without fear of harassment. Related was the question of the proper venue for political speech. Was the classroom to be off limits? Was the commons building? For the constituency, the issue was often a theological and religious question. The Democratic Party was frequently tarred with the brush of "socialism," and socialism was considered anti-Christian. If professors were members of the Democratic Party, the argument went, they were violating their confessional integrity. Moreover, since the constituency continued to look upon Calvin as "our school," they felt disappointed and betrayed when professors departed from traditionally accepted views. And some of the constituency were not loath to express their disappointment.

I find it heartening that the board and administration did not succumb to the more extreme demands of some churches and church members to "clean house." The faculty members were allowed to explain their positions and were not muzzled. The 1962 statement, "Political Activities of Professors," is a prudent policy, guarding freedom of speech while also counseling discretion.

15 *Reformed Journal*, May-June, 1965, 23.

16 The Canadian segment of the CRC was generally much more tolerant of political diversity. The Canadian church consisted largely of immigrants from the Netherlands, where there was much more openness to governmental involvement in social and economic areas, as there was in their newly adopted country, Canada.

The Creation-Evolution Storm

One of the most severe conflicts between college and church was the creation-evolution conflict, lasting roughly from 1984 to 1991. The writings of three science professors occasioned a storm of protests in the church, and the conflict was one of the significant reasons for the departure of dozens of congregations and thousands of members from the denomination. I will deal with this matter at some length for several reasons. First, the issue of creation and evolution is a critical theological and scientific question, both in the CRC and in other denominations. Second, creation/evolution controversies have been the frequent cause for conflicts between academic and church communities. Calvin College's controversy is therefore of historical interest. Third, after the 1991 synodical report, "Creation and Science," there has been very little formal discussion on creation and evolution in either the CRC or Calvin College. Neither has there been, to my knowledge, an overview of this controversy. No doubt many of the participants were battle weary, but the questions require ongoing discussion. Fourth, the evolution-creation controversy displayed, perhaps more than any other debate, the intertwining of church and school.[17]

It would be an oversimplification to say that the controversy started with a *Banner* article, but certainly for many people that article brought the issue to the fore. In an interview, Clarence Menninga, chairman of the Calvin College Geology Department, testified,

"I believe that God created this universe. I also believe that God upholds and sustains and controls it—all good, Calvinistic affirmations." But he went on to assert a number of other issues:

17 There had been earlier rumblings about professors teaching evolution. In the 1960s Donald Wilson, professor of sociology and anthropology, was questioned about his views on creation. In the early 1970s, Willis De Boer, professor in the Religion and Theology Department, was grilled about his interpretation of Genesis. Interestingly, the 1948 publication of *Beyond the Atom* by John De Vries, professor of chemistry at Calvin, did not provoke much controversy, even though he advocated an "old earth"; the old earth theory was attacked in the controversy under discussion.

The earth is probably several billion years old, Adam may have been a Neanderthal, and man may have been around for forty thousand years. Moreover, those, like the Scientific Creationists, who hold to an earth of six thousand years and fiat creation, base their conclusions on superficialities, and "sometimes their arguments ignore important information that bears on the discussion."[18]

The December 17 issue of *The Banner* carried the first letters of disapproval, and President Diekema, the Board of Trustees, and Menninga soon began to receive the beginning of an avalanche of responses. One of the briefest letters made its point forcefully:

> You suggest that Adam had neighbors when he was born? Actually you said "maybe."
>
> In a Christian Reformed College we may not have that kind of misleading and false direction. For Christians the supernatural act of God's creation is a true fact. Are you saying that God has fooled us all these years?
>
> Remember Dr. Menninga the commandment "thou shalt have no other Gods before me." It seems to me that the God of science supersedes God supernatural. I am asking you Dr. Menninga to repent and change your view. Please let me know by return mail so that I may know for certain and take appropriate steps to fight false teachings in our denomination.[19]

The Events. Since much of the evolution discussion came to center on the term "the event character" (especially of Genesis 1), I will designate this section "The Events"—to sketch the chronology of the controversy. Many of the details will be supplied in later sections.

Prior to the Menninga interview, Davis Young of the Geology Department had published *Christianity and the Age of the Earth*. In the book Young took a fairly traditional stance, but he did hold to an

[18] "Creation and Geology," *The Banner*, November 12, 1984, 10.
[19] Diekema Papers, Creation vs. Evolution, February 13, 1985.

"old earth" theory: "...the doctrine of the evolution of man is unscriptural and should be opposed. Christians should not, however, attempt to disprove evolutionary theory by discrediting the antiquity of the Earth."[20] The book also contained trenchant criticism of adherents of Creation Science. Critique of the book was muted at the time of publication, but critics frequently cited the book later.

The Menninga interview in 1984 prompted the beginning of more severe censure of the geology professors, and this criticism grew voluminous (and often acrimonious) with the publication of (physics professor) Howard Van Till's *The Fourth Day*.[21] By 1987 the college administration and the board became sufficiently alarmed to form a committee to investigate the matter. The mandate of the committee was to study and evaluate the views of the three professors "...and to determine whether these statements are in accord with the synodically adopted guidelines for the interpretation of Scripture and with the doctrinal statements of the Christian Reformed Church." (The committee was never christened with a proper name; it remained "the *Ad Hoc* Committee".) The committee's conclusions and report[22] were greeted with considerable fanfare. This was probably the only committee in the history of the college that elicited a press conference, as well as coverage in the *Detroit Free Press*. The *Ad Hoc* Committee's report and the board of trustees' report to synod 1988 were generally supportive of the professors, and the trustees presented the report as its "Recommendations which may serve as answers to the various communications received by the board" (*Agenda for Synod*, 1988, 23). However, between February and June, the synodical office received thirty-one overtures—nearly all highly censorious of the report. (The usual route in CRC polity is for a congregation to present an overture, expressing the congregation's charge or

[20] Davis A. Young, *Christianity and the Age of the Earth* (Grand Rapids: Zondervan, 1982), 66.

[21] Howard J. Van Till, *The Fourth Day: What the Bible and the Heavens Are Telling us about the Creation* (Grand Rapids: Eerdmans, 1986).

[22] Report to the Board of Trustees, February 8, 1988.

recommendation, to its classis. If the classis agrees with the overture, classis can adopt it as its own and send it to synod; if classis does not adopt it, the congregation can send the overture directly to synod). At its June meeting, synod engaged in vigorous (six-hour) debate and, with some reservations, officially endorsed the work of both committee and board (*Acts*, 1988, 597-98). Synod also followed an honorable tradition—it established a study committee which was mandated to study especially the relationship between general and special revelation. However, protests versus the report continued, as some of the press, as we will see later in this chapter, was vociferous in its denunciation.

The professors added fuel to the fire by their publication of *Science Held Hostage*.[23] Although the essays were written in 1984-85, the publication at this time confirmed to the critics that the science professors were not faithful to the Christian tradition. This critique was occasioned especially by the professors' vigorous criticism of Scientific Creationism, a perspective admired by most of the conservative critics.

The study committee appointed by synod 1988 reported in 1991 with a lengthy and thorough report, "Creation and Science" (*Agenda for Synod*, 367-433). This time synod debated for eight hours—much of it focused on a minority recommendation (Declaration F) that "the church declares that the clear teaching of Scripture and of our confessions on the uniqueness of human beings as image bearers of God rules out all theories that posit the reality of evolutionary forebears of the human race" (410). Synod, however, refused to accept this statement, largely on the grounds that the CRC had never made an official pronouncement on the scientific details of creation. That same year a new "Special Committee" of the the college's board of trustees presented its final report, largely expressing confidence in the professors and refusing to limit their teaching and research.

23 Howard J. Van Till, Davis A. Young, Clarence Menninga, *Science Held Hostage* (Downers Grove, IL: InterVarsity Press, 1988).

Synod 1991 still received twenty-four overtures—mostly critical of Van Till's views—but these overtures were now in competition with the thirty-eight overtures against women in ecclesiastical office. By 1992 this number was reduced to three, and two final overtures in 1994 were the last blip on the synodical screen. The church seemed to signal that the storm was over.

The Dispute. Nearly ten years of controversy produced a flood of lectures, articles, editorials, books, letters to the editor, speeches at synod, and paid advertisements. The issue was multiform and complex; the disciplines ranged from astronomy to zoology, from Hebrew grammar to biblical hermeneutics; the authors included concerned church members, learned scholars, and beleaguered administrators; the passions often ran high. Trying to reduce that tangled history to a few pages is a perilous undertaking, but it is worth trying to discern the main outlines of the dispute.

In delineating the arguments of the professors, I will ignore the rich detail of their presentations and will take their learning and scholarship for granted. It is worth noting that they had served the college, and the Christian academic world, for many years. Menninga and Van Till began teaching at Calvin in 1967 and Young in 1978. I will lament only in passing that their many years of scholarly contributions and classroom teaching often became reduced to one contentious issue.

In sketching the three scientists' views, one must begin by positing that they firmly believed in the creation of the cosmos by a sovereign God and in God's continuing upholding of the universe. They firmly renounced what is usually called materialistic evolutionism—the philosophy that the universe came into being by random physical forces and processes.

They differed in their explanation of divine creation from the interpretation held by nearly all of Christendom till about 1850 and still held by many fundamentalist and evangelical Christians today. The scientists' explanation held that the age of the universe must be billions of years (rather than the traditional 6,000-10,000 years); that the creation did not occur in six twenty-four hour days but involved a process lasting billions of years; and that human beings may have been part of that process. In addition, the flood of Genesis 7-8 was not a worldwide deluge, but a more local occurrence. Their views were buttressed by studies in geology, astronomy, biology, and anthropology. These explanations, the scientists said, might run counter to more traditional interpretations of Scripture, but were not in violation of biblical truth, nor of the creeds of the CRC.

Van Till especially explicated in more detail how their interpretation was not at variance with biblical revelation—rightly interpreted. Much of *The Fourth Day* was devoted to a construal of reading Genesis 1-11 as primeval history, which does not bind us to a reportorial interpretation. Another crucial theory of Van Till was the notion that in the biblical story we must distinguish between vehicle and message, or form and content. The vehicle is the literary genre that carries the message. Finally, science and Scripture have quite different tasks and aims. Science's task is to investigate and describe the material world; such scientific research opens up God's general revelation in nature. Scripture teaches us that the cosmos is God's creation and that he has established a covenant with mankind and the rest of creation. These two sources ask different questions, but they complement each other.

Let me also try to summarize the position of the traditionalists. Here my summary is even more risky, since we have (counting letters to the Calvin board and administration) hundreds of writers. But a number of basic issues kept reappearing.

The first chapter of Genesis teaches clearly that God created the world by fiat. God said, "Let there be...," and that pronouncement immediately brought forth the universe—in six twenty-four hour days and nights. (I realize that not all the traditionalists insisted on the six literal days). Next, biblical history teaches that this creation (including the creation of Adam and Eve) took place approximately six thousand years ago. The special creation of man (the traditionalists were generally quite content to leave Eve out of the picture) must especially be safeguarded. The strongest reaction against the scientists came whenever there was even an intimation that humanity evolved from a "lower" animal form. Another objection was voiced against the scientists' theory that the great flood was local. Since Genesis 7 clearly speaks of "all flesh" and "the earth," it is obvious that the flood was worldwide. Besides disagreement about the interpretation of specific texts in Genesis, there was strong reaction against Van Till's characterization of Genesis 1-11 as "primeval history." Instead, these chapters are to be read as reportage of what actually took place at the beginning of creation and the beginning of history. The scientists' claim that the evidence of general revelation complements the special revelation of Scripture must also be qualified. Both the created world and our understanding of that world have been ravaged by sin, and one must therefore never put general and special revelation on equal footing.

These, then, were some of the major issues that divided the scientists from the more traditional interpretation. Let me assert again that both points of view were presented in fine detail, with scholarly finesse, and (usually) with great passion.

The Critics. In summarizing the critics of the three scientists we will look mostly at the writings against Professor Van Till, since much of the censure was directed at him. However, the intent usually was to encompass Menninga and Young if their views overlapped with Van Till's. Although I will mostly survey the negative reviews of Van Till's *The Fourth Day*, such were not the only evaluations. Both theologians and other scientists praised the book highly. *Perspectives* lauded the book, because it "provides a clear and readily understood summary of the informed evangelical position today: a position dedicated to the upholding of authentic biblical theology and authentic science."[24] Even the conservative *Westminster Theological Journal* commended *The Fourth Day* for its critique of Creation

24 Richard H. Bube, "Review," *Perspectives: Journal of the American Scientific Affiliation* 38, 3 (September 1986): 215.

Science, although the reviewer does find fault with Van Till.[25] Here I will survey primarily reviews from the CRC community, with a concentration on those which were negative.

We will begin with one of the best discussions between Van Till and a colleague-critic—the exchanges in *Christian Scholars Review.*[26] Alvin Plantinga, professor of philosophy at the University of Notre Dame (formerly at Calvin College), presented a lengthy essay, "When Faith and Reason Clash: Evolution and the Bible." Van Till (and two other scholars) responded, and Plantinga answered their responses.

In his essay, Plantinga agreed with Van Till on a number of issues, including the probability of an "ancient earth." But he also disagreed vigorously on other questions. He found the probability of the "grand evolutionary story" and the theory of "common ancestry" highly suspect and tending to be inimical to Christian doctrine. In many ways he was also very sympathetic to the Creation Science proponents. Van Till in turn agreed with Plantinga in many areas but continued to differ strongly in others. What strikes one in this exchange is the tone of mutual respect, of courtesy, of trust. One could only wish that more of the discussion had exhibited that spirit.

The most extensive commentary on Van Till's views from a colleague was by Henry Vander Goot, at the time a professor in the Religion and Theology Department (Vander Goot left Calvin in 1992). In a 133-page typescript, "From Illusion to Restriction," Vander Goot presented a hard-hitting criticism of *The Fourth Day.* In his critique he challenged Van Till on a number of fundamental issues, such as the form-content distinction, the notion that the Bible deals only (or primarily) with a "religious" domain, and ascribing a largely "neutral" stance to scientific investigation. Moreover, Vander Goot stressed that the biblical principle of separation, division, or distinction is at odds with Van Till's

25 Robert C. Newman, "Review," *Westminster Journal* 48, 2 (Fall, 1986): 410-12.
26 *Christian Scholar's Review* 21, 1 (September 1991):8-45.

conception of development and evolution. Overall, Vander Goot judged Van Till's views to be a dangerous synthesis of biblical truth and evolutionary science. He concluded, "My impression is that unbeknownst to the author, ironically, scholasticism and not Calvinism shapes much of the tone, character, and structure of *Fourth Day*, even though the content of VT's thinking is evolutionary and anti-scholastic."[27]

Scrutiny also came directly from the churches. Criticism from particular congregations was, in some ways, the most telling, since they represented a crucial segment of the denomination. Of course, one cannot assume that each statement from a congregation spoke for all in that church. A clique, or a segment of the church council, or a zealous pastor might be more responsible for a point of view than a whole congregation. The trustees files contain correspondence with dozens of congregations; in some cases the correspondence covers eight years. Another frequent expression of congregational voice was the overture. Between 1988 and 1994, there were some seventy overtures dealing with the creation-evolution debate; nearly all of these were critical of the views of the scientists or of the handling of the situation by a previous synod or by the Calvin Board of Trustees.

Some of the overtures were terse statements. Classis Minnesota North merely asked synod to reaffirm that "We believe that God created man from the dust of the earth and made and formed him in his image and likeness" (*Agenda for Synod*, 1994, 280). Others were lengthy disputations: Classis Zeeland submitted a seven-page, closely argued, report in 1988 (*Acts*, 1988, 443-49). Occasionally congregations made use of boiler plate overtures—those that had been formulated and circulated by like-minded authors.

The periodical press also became very involved. *Christian Renewal* (*CR*) became one of the most persistent and severe critics. Published in Canada, the magazine had been a caustic voice about developments

[27] Henry Vander Goot, "From Illusion to Restriction" (Printed at Calvin College, 1989), 130.

in the CRC, and it helped galvanize a secessionist movement from the denomination. *CR* shot its opening salvo in the March 4, 1985, issue. Eleven pages were devoted to the creation-evolution question, much of it directed at professors George Marsden (who had testified in court for the ACLU), Menninga, and Young. In the editor's article, the tenor of the debate was clear from the outset: "*Hubris*, academic pride and a saturation of secular learning at state universities has turned the learned professors against the revealed Word of God."[28] In a subsequent issue the three professors responded with an "Open Letter," decrying the accusations, appealing to Abraham Kuyper, and holding that they stood in the orthodox, Reformed corner with Warfield, Bavinck, Machen, and Hodge.[29]

The scientists' letter obviously did not persuade the critics, since *CR* persisted with a continuing barrage, ranging from carefully argued pieces to scurrilous accusation. One of the longest contributions was a series by Lester De Koster. In nine articles (March 23-September 21, 1987) he reviewed *The Fourth Day*. De Koster's stance was clear from the start:

> Let it be plainly said that in this reviewer's judgment, this book is so flagrantly and deceptively at odds with the Bible that if it be allowed to stand as representative of teaching on the Calvin campus, the Board of Trustees has reason to wonder what claim it has left on the trust of its constituency....*The Fourth Day* is an exercise in short-changing the Bible—and in covering up the biblical accounts which contradict the fraud.[30]

The series continued with a zealous restatement of the traditional interpretation of the creation story, challenging Van Till especially

28 John Hultink, "What Are We to Do with Adam and Eve, *Christian Renewal,* March 4, 1985, 8.

29 May 20, 1985, 6.

30 March 23, 1987, 7.

on his interpretation of Scripture. Throughout the series the argument was buttressed by De Koster's rhetorical thrusts and parries, irony, and sarcasm.[31]

Editor Hultink also continued his offensive. He penned a "Dear Calvin College Students" letter, providing the students with questions and answers to challenge and contradict their evolutionist professors. To whet the students' desire, Hultink offered a "reward" of $10,000 (in American funds, no less) to any students who could elicit from one of the professors "one iota of scientific proof in support of evolution."[32] Jelle Tuininga, a well known conservative pastor, when commenting on an interview with Van Till in the June 1987 *Calvin Spark*, warned against "blind institutional loyalty, which is a form of idolatry."[33]Another issue blasted with quadruple-barreled headlines. Hultink entitled his piece, "Howard Van Till Dishonest"; Lester De Koster weighed in with a critique of the Board of Trustees Report with, "Darwinese is Spoken Here"; Jelle Tuininga added his opprobrium of Davis Young's speech at Calvin Seminary with, "Spreading Evolutionary Speculation to the Seminary"; and there was a full-page reproduction of Leo Peter's advertisement in the *Grand Rapids Press*,[34] "Calvin teaches biblical Creation is false."[35]

31 This author is the same De Koster who was attacked by the constituency when he was a professor at Calvin.

32 September 7, 1987, 12.

33 August 10, 1987, 2 and 17.

34 Mr. Leo Peters, a Grand Rapids inventor and entrepeneur, will probably earn a permanent footnote in the annals of the Christian Reformed Church and Calvin College. He was alternately perceived as a defender of the faith or as a religious fanatic. Peters gained his fame with a series of full-page advertisements the *Grand Rapids Press*—usually in the Saturday Religion section.

One of the early ads set the tone: "[Van Till's] book is the most flagrant example of deceitful scholarship I've ever seen. Its gross claims are neither good Christianity, nor good science.... But now, in granting academic freedom on biblical matters to the professors of Calvin College & Seminary the Trustees have in fact declared that this CRC-owned institution is no longer Christian..." In the same tirade, the Reverend Andrew Kuyvenhoven, editor of *The Banner*, was called "an avowed secular humanist" (*Grand Rapids Press*, March 19, 1988, D6). Later that year, Peters upped the ante with a double-page advertisement which included a section "DDD&K: THE FOUR HORSEMEN OF THE APOCALYPSE." The designated destroyers were President

By 1990 Hultink admitted that the *CR* combat had not worked, and he saw only one solution: "...the problem worsens. And will continue to worsen until Anthony Diekema is asked to resign as president of Calvin College."[36] A few weeks later his headline read: "Lying to Save an Institution."[37] The 1991 synodical report, "Creation and Science," was also thoroughly thrashed. Jelle Tuininga concluded that the decisions of the report "completely eliminated the possibility of ever dismissing any professors or scientists who believed in the evolutionary development of the human race, and that was the clear intent of this amendment. It made sure that no heads would roll."[38]

The College. From the previous discussion it is obvious that the college was at times consumed by the issue. Faculty and student reaction tended to come to the surface at critical times and was nearly uniformly supportive of the faculty members. However, a report by the Professional Status Committee ("Procedures for

Diekema of the college, President De Jong of the seminary, the Reverend Charles De Ridder, president of the board of trustees, and Kuyvenhoven of *The Banner.* For good measure, Peters added two strategists and henchmen who supplied ammunition in the destruction of the church: Howard Van Till, and John Bratt, professor of religion at the college. Peters could imagine that some readers might find his characterization extreme—but be not deceived: "Behind their respectable facades they are hard-boiled and ruthless, riding rough-shod over the 'naïve' (ignorant) CRC members who refuse to sacrifice their faith in God's authority for faith in DDD&K's authority" [*Grand Rapids Press*, November 26, 1988, C5]. And so it continued for a dozen more ads of vitriol. (James Bratt delivered a lecture in the 1989 "January Lectures" series, entitled "Cotton Mather, Joseph McCarthy, Leo Peters and the Hunt for Witches." This was reprinted in the February 1989 *Dialogue*. It was a brilliant expose of Peters in the context of other periods in American history).

Peters's influence is rather difficult to gauge. Those who tended to agree with him appreciated the visibility he gave to the cause but were often embarrassed by the personal attacks and the coarse language. The college was embarrassed by the dirty linen displayed to all the subscribers of the *Press*, and Peters's home church didn't quite know what to do with their disputatious member. It is doubtful if the time and money Peters spent on the ads influenced the outcome of the controversy in any significant way; his campaign certainly did not contribute to any meaningful dialogue.

35 April 11, 1988.

36 October 23, 1990, 2.

37 November 26, 1990, 2.

38 July 15, 1991, 8.

handling allegations of confessional unorthodoxy," November 21, 1991) did note that "the process did not involve collegial support of Professor Van Till in any formal or specific way."[39] Here we will look briefly at the "official" voice of the college, as it came to expression through the administration and the board of trustees.

The administration was involved through the offices of college relations, the provost, and the president. The controversy was, of course, a nightmare for public relations. The censorious synodical discussions, the letters from irate church members and congregations, the choleric editorials from the church press, and the acrimonious ads from Leo Peters had the college relations department working arduously to contain the damage. At one point the College Relations Committee sent detailed recommendations to President Diekema, outlining specific steps to deal with the controversy. Many of the recommendations dealt with communication, and strongly urged the board to communicate more promptly and fully with the churches.[40] Although the provost, Gordon Van Harn, generally worked in the background, he did speak out on the issue, defending the professors' viewpoint. In a joint interview with Diekema, Van Harn defended his professors, both on the grounds of academic freedom and on their remaining within confessional bounds.[41] The president's office was involved in the issue from the beginning. After the initial letters protesting Menninga's *Banner* interview, Diekema's mail basket continued to be crammed with constituents' missives (often including the threat or announcement that the sender would no longer support the college financially), and dutifully answered all of them. Toward the end of the controversy, Diekema praised the synodical study committee report as one "which should guide both the college and the church in the months and years ahead."[42] On the issue of Van

39 See "President's Report to the BOT," February 13, 1992, 55.
40 "College Relations Committee Advisory Report," Decembert 13, 1988.
41 *Calvin Spark,* September, 1988, 20-24.
42 "Supplementary Report to the Board of Trustees,"August 28, 1991.

Till, he concluded, "Although wearied by it, we are grateful for the careful and deliberate way in which the church and the Synod have now resolved the matter."[43]

Obviously, the Calvin College Board of Trustees played a pivotal role in the controversy. Surveying the archives' files of the board, it becomes quickly evident that the creation-evolution controversy demanded an extraordinary amount of discussion and correspondence time. Although the investigative task was assigned to committees, the executive committee of the board and the full board also spent a vast amount of time discussing the conflict. (Daniel Vander Ark, secretary of the board, begins one of his letters to a fellow board member with, "These are the times that try trustees' souls"). The work of the *Ad Hoc* Committee has been referred to above. After the release of that committee's report in February 1988, the board established another committee in November of that year. (This committee never received a proper moniker either; it continued to be called "the Special Committee.") Its mandate was to give scriptural direction and pastoral advice to the professors and to work toward clarification about ambiguous issues.

The committee's task was not easy and its course did not run smoothly. Its first report was sent in a letter to church councils. The views of Menninga and Young were judged to be "within the bounds of our creedal forms of unity," and the committee was "satisfied" with their views. For Van Till, however, "there remain matters at this time that are inconclusive and unresolved with respect to some of his views. Therefore, the Board intends for its committee to deal further with them."[44] By May, 1990, the committee had lost unanimity and submitted two reports. One report judged

43 Diekema's evaluation of the creation-evolution controversy is voiced most clearly in his recently published book, *Academic Freedom and Christian Scholarship.* He finds the opponents of the college to use "innuendo, distortion, and blatant untruth, they move to create unrest in the church and constituency in efforts to gain supporters to their 'cause'" (121).

44 Letter of BOT to Councils of the CRCNA, February 21, 1990.

that "the Board should not place Howard Van Till under any special restrictions as a Calvin professor at this time." The other report had serious misgivings about Van Till, especially "his reluctance to affirm that Adam and Eve were specific historical individuals," his view of Scripture, and his reservations about the Form of Subscription.[45] By February, 1991, the committee did come with a unified report, and this report was distributed to the churches. One of the principal recommendations was "...that the Board of Trustees acknowledge with gratitude Professor Howard Van Till's concurrence with the conclusions of the committee's written report and with confidence attest to his faithfulness to the promises he made in signing the Form of Subscription, his submission to the authority of the written Word of God, and his avowal of the historicity of the Adam and Eve of Scripture."[46]

Conclusion. Why did the church (or at least a segment of the church) react so violently? Several factors came into play. First, the timing. By 1985 the CRC had already experienced great disharmony. The issue of women in ecclesiastical office had caused friction since the early 1970s, questions of biblical hermeneutics and interpretation often simmered under the surface, and the conservative wing of the church was noisily restive. A number of individual congregations had already begun to leave the denomination, and there was increasing talk of "secession."

Moreover, both Calvin College and Calvin Seminary had suffered erosion of support and trust for a number of years. For example, in the 1960s the seminary and the church were embroiled in a five-year controversy about the views of Professor Harold Dekker. Twenty years later the church protested the appointment of Professor Henry De Moor. So with the college. One local congregation challenged the views of Professor Willis De Boer of the Religion and Theology Department for six years. Again, "Report 44" ("The Nature of and Extent of Biblical Authority," *Acts*, 1972, 493-546)

45 "Special Committee Report to BOT," May 1, 1990.
46 "Report of the Special Committee to the BOT," February, 1991, 20.

was considered the beginning of the end of doctrinal fidelity by conservatives; five of its six authors were professors at CalvinCollege and Seminary. A more general distrust was spawned in the sixties, when rebellious students and radical faculty created a rift between church and academia—a rift of suspicion that continued for many years. The Association of Christian Reformed Laymen had been sniping (in anonymous fashion) at Calvin College and Seminary since 1965, and many students (or their parents) opted for colleges other than Calvin—colleges considered more conservative and safe.

It is hazardous to characterize a large segment of a church, but I will hazard that the conservative wing of the CRC was more conservative in 1980 than in 1960. (Of course, the folks representing that group might contend that they only *appeared* to be more conservative because the denomination as a whole had shifted to a more liberal position). The interpretation of Genesis 1 is a case in point. The notion that the "day" in the creation story had to be a "literal" day of twenty-four hours had never been a litmus test of orthodoxy. However, among conservatives this view became increasingly dominant, especially as the influence of the Creation Science movement became more pronounced. (This drift toward rigid conservatism can also be plotted in the history after the period under consideration: those who left the CRC and joined the United Reformed Church made this view semiofficial church policy in 1999.)

Thus the stage was set for a conflict of major proportion, and the creation-evolution debate became the most critical controversy in the history of Calvin College. Moreover, the dispute revealed the often convoluted intertwining of church and college as few other issues did.

The controversy was protracted and painful for both church and college. I have discussed and cited the "far right" in the debate, where scurrilous accusations were used as often as genuine arguments. However, there were also many congregations and church members who did not stoop to such polemics, but who were deeply involved and affected. Church members saw a departure from Scripture and they felt betrayed by their leadership. Many continued their membership in the CRC, while many others left. Those who cited reasons for leaving the CRC often included that "the CRC tolerates the teaching of theistic evolution, including the denial of a world wide flood in the time of Noah" or some such phrase.

For the college the controversy was a wrenching episode, consuming an incredible amount of time and energy. Although I have not discussed the plight of the professors in any detail, the debate was often an agonizing experience for them, as they were accused of heresy, disloyalty to Scripture, and being a menace to the faith. They spent untold hours explaining and defending their positions to the board and its committees, and they traveled to many churches to explain their views about science and the Bible.

More positively, the college solidified its relationship with many alumni and supporters. Those who agreed with the views of the professors became more firm in their allegiance to Calvin. The college also defined anew the nature of Christian academic inquiry and the contours of such inquiry in relation to the church and its confessions. A specific document originating from the controversy was a "Procedure for cases in which the Board of Trustees receives Allegations of Confessional Unorthodoxy against faculty members" (BOT Minutes, February 13-14, 1992, Art. 25). In the "Procedure," a prominent role is assigned to the provost and the Professional Status Committee, and the process is to be much more expeditious than was the case with Van Till.

Although the controversy was painful for the denomination, the discussions and decisions did help to clarify a number of issues, and the CRC defined anew the limits of its theological diversity. The 1991 report, "Creation and Science," especially in its approach to general and special revelation, notably elucidated the permissibility of various interpretations of the creation account.

Coda on Professors

As I did with the closing section on students in the previous chapter, so I need to revisit the relationship between the Calvin College faculty and the CRC constituency. The focus of this chapter has been on the criticism of the faculty and their views, and the resulting strain between school and church. Here, again, that criticism must be seen in the context of nearly 125 years of appreciation and mutual benefit. Let me count some of the ways in which Calvin professors have interacted with the Christian Reformed Church.

The most direct influence on the church has been the post-secondary education of tens of thousands of students who have in countless ways contributed to the life of the denomination. Even though I do not wish to discount the impact of the other CRC-related colleges in the past forty years (or the education of those who studied elsewhere), it remains true that Calvin College alumni have had a major influence on the church. A great number of pastors, teachers, other professionals, as well as people who serve church and community in countless ways were trained and guided by generations of Calvin professors.

The writing, lecturing, and consulting of the faculty outside the classroom has always been substantial. Much of this writing has been for academic and professional audiences (such as a psychology professor presenting a lecture on autism), and may be of only indirect significance for the church. But much writing has also been aimed more directly at the church. Books from Calvin authors have poured from pen, typewriter, and computer ever since the college's origin, from B.K. Kuiper, *Ons Opmaken en Bouwen* (1918), to Enno Wolthuis, *Science, God, and You* (1963), to Shirley Roels, *Christians and Economic Life* (1990). The Christian school movement has benefited enormously from the contributions of Calvin authors; Jacob Van den Bosch wrote *Our Schools—What They Are and What They Should Be* in 1914, and Gloria Goris Stronks published *A Vision With a Task* in 1993. In between those dates many education books, articles, lectures, consultations, and speeches at Christian school conventions have been offered unstintingly by Calvin faculty. If one glances through the indexes of *The Banner* and other periodicals, one will find hundreds of Calvin authors. Again, the molding of the CRC community has not been performed only by Calvin professors, but certainly their contribution has been significant and enduring.

In western Michigan the Calvin influence has been especially noticeable. Calvin faculty have served faithfully on school boards and church councils, filled pulpits, and participated in the education programs of local churches, in addition to carrying out many other civic responsibilities.

As suggested before, this cordial and beneficial relationship between college and denomination does not cloak the strife discussed earlier in this chapter or the significance of that strife for both college and church. But the discord must be seen in the context of widespread accord.

8

Retrospect and Prospect

One of my earlier chapters is entitled, "What's the Matter with Calvin?" The clichéd answer is, of course, "It depends on whom you ask." We have heard a number of voices of those who found much amiss with Calvin College. Faculty writing on evolution or having the "wrong" political affiliation, students traveling on Sundays or protesting the Vietnam War or writing outrageous articles, the administration not enforcing the movies ban or admitting non-CRC students—all of these transgressions were duly noted and objected to by various parties in the CRC.

At the same time, others throughout this history responded, "There's nothing much wrong with Calvin; we're proud of our school." Surveying Calvin's 125 years of existence, one is struck by the remarkable support from alumni and the church at large. As I have noted several times, even though this study has often focused on points of tension and conflict, the overall history is one of loyal cooperation between church and school.

I will here make some concluding remarks about this relationship and suggest some future directions. First, let me sum up some of the causes for the tensions between the CRC and Calvin College.

Causes of Tension

Ownership and Control. I know of no college or university that is always in accord with its supporting constituency or its trustees. Whether the "owners" be a state legislature, wealthy benefactors, a Baptist convention, or a Reformed denomination—there will always be a measure of strain and conflict. Such tension is unavoidable. If a constituency is largely responsible for the financial support of a college, such donors will wish to see a reflection of their own political, theological, or social visions in the college. A denominational college is certainly prone to such pressures. In the case of a denomination such as the CRC, which has had and continues to have a strong confessional tradition, the desire for theological consonance between church and college will remain firm.

Moreover, by their very nature church and school will often be in conflict. A denomination frequently represents convention and tradition. The church seeks to pass on beliefs and values of previous generations, and its worship life will maintain the customary rituals. A college may reflect such denominational values, but it will also seek to push the boundaries of knowledge, expand the world of learning, and explore new intellectual horizons. This search for scientific advances or bold new theories will often produce collisions with the church. Students also contribute to the potential conflict. They often express their independence from home and church during their college years, and their independence has often not (yet) matured into wisdom.

The Christian college and its supporting church may also have different views on the relationship between church and world, and between faith and learning. The church will frequently stress separation from its surrounding culture, while the college will be caught up in the disciplines of science or literature, where the very nature of education demands immersion in such fields.

Finally, a church college is vulnerable to denominational divisions. As several Calvin presidents lamented, the church struggles were sometimes fought on college turf. The movie controversy is perhaps the clearest example of this tendency. Since the CRC retained an official ban on all movie attendance till 1966, the college was forced to police student attendance much longer than if the church had not had the ban.

Historical Reasons. The personality and history of the CRC also contributed to the strain between church and school. The CRC had its origin in several major church secessions, in 1834 and 1886 in the Netherlands and in 1857 in America. Such splits promote a sensitivity to doctrinal purity, but also a spirit of suspicion. I don't know who first applied the adage "rotten wood doesn't split" to church life, but one can well imagine that some CRC dogmatic worthies agree with the sentiment. An unyielding zeal for truth, they contend, may produce strife, but such strife (and even church splits) may be necessary.

The presence of the three dominant theological streams delineated in chapter 2 may have contributed to discord as well. It is, no doubt, possible to be an ardent pietist, a doctrinaire confessionalist, and a zealous Kuyperian transformer of culture—all at the same time in one person. But often these emphases were at odds with each other and produced strife in both church and college and between church and college.

The history of the CRC and of Calvin College is also a history of immigration, of ethnic identity, and of Americanization. Such a history usually produces questions and disagreements about issues such as language change, religious traditions, worship patterns, political involvement, customs, dress, education, marriage, and a host of other matters. Sometimes an issue was one of adoption ("Should we sing hymns as the Methodists do?"), at other times one of pace ("When should we no longer have Dutch services?"). But the identity of being Dutch-Americans often contributed to the disputes. Moreover, the immigrants were usually those with limited education and from lower socio-economic strata—thus often suspicious of the ways of college students and professors.

Organizational Structure. The organizational structure of Calvin contributed to potential friction as well. The CRC carried on a decades-long debate over whether it was appropriate for the church to own and operate a college. No matter how strong and persuasive the opposition was at times, the synodical answer always was, "Yes!" This periodic affirmation became a constant reminder that Calvin College belonged to and was owned by the church, with the implicit or explicit addendum, "and the college must give account to the church." This sense of ownership and accountability was reinforced by the membership of the board of trustees—until 1948 board membership was restricted to CRC ministers, and until 1992 to CRC members. The financial support of the college further contributed to the sense of church ownership. Although the percentage of the college budget contributed by the church decreased over the years, the required assessments via quotas and ministry shares added to the notion "We pay for the college and therefore should have a say in what's going on there."

Finally, the composition of student body and faculty so strengthened the ties between church and school that at times the church regarded the college as an adjunct of the denomination. As late as 1970 CRC students accounted for 92 percent of the student body, and virtually all (tenured) faculty had to join the CRC. Such composition continued to portray the school as an institution of and for "our people." The college was often seen as an extension of the church, thus ignoring the fact that a church and an educational institution have different functions. As Diekema correctly notes, "Antagonism between the church and the college...tends to be caused by losing sight of their different yet complementary tasks."[1] Diekema then cites Roman Catholic colleges and universities as an example, but this confusion of tasks was equally true of Calvin College and the Christian Reformed Church. Indeed, if Diekema's "Modest Proposals"[2] for church colleges had been operative in the

[1] Diekema, *Academic Freedom,* 116.
[2] Ibid., 115-43.

history of Calvin, many of the controversies between church and school would not have occurred.

The Church as Anchor

When considering the benefits to Calvin of being a "church college," one thinks, of course, of the generous support of the denomination. In the early years, virtually all of the financial support came from the CRC constituency, either through the required quotas, financial "drives," or student tuition. Although the required quota amount has decreased in terms of the percentage of the total college budget, support from CRC constituency continues to be an important factor. More intangible support in terms of prayer, encouragement, collaboration, time, and many other means of assistance are as important to the college today as in 1900.

Another way to see the influence of the CRC on Calvin College is in its religious, confessional moorings. If one reviews the history of Christian higher education in North America, the landscape is often rather bleak. A very large number of colleges and universities have left their religious traditions and have become thoroughly secular.[3] Even if one does not believe in historical determinism, the danger of secularization is a real one for all Christian colleges, especially if they become respected and "successful" in the general academic world. "There but for the grace of God. . ." is an appropriate thought for any church college. One reason that Calvin has, by and large, retained its confessional identity and integrity is its affiliation with the CRC. Through the board, the annual synods, and the broader constituency the college has always been aware of an orthodox heritage and been accountable to a confessional community. No doubt the college at times regarded the church as an albatross, but ultimately the denomination's influence has been beneficial. Several nautical images come to mind. At various times the church served as ballast, keeping the college from flighty

[3] See especially George Marsden, *The Soul of the University,* and James Burtchaell, *The Dying of the Light.*

experiments, or as a buoy, signaling dangerous shoals, or as a compass, showing direction, or as a rudder, steering on an *ortho* (straight) path, or perhaps, as K. Galbraith says in another context, "as a firm anchor in nonsense." Both the common-sense restraints of church members (frequently with very little formal education) and the well-honed critiques of disapproving theologues forced Calvin to scrutinize its decisions and directions carefully.

An Expanded Statement of the Mission of Calvin College captures well the role of the church at its best:

> The church provides the college with a definitive Reformed legacy, an articulation of one tradition in the exercise of Christian faith. It brings this distinctiveness to the college in a theological heritage that antedates the founding of the college, that has shaped the history of the college, and that continues to provide a framework for the activities of the college. Moreover, within biblical authority and in its interpretation of Reformed distinctiveness, the church supplies the college with a moral framework for Christian living and ethical decision-making.[4]

Today and Tomorrow

The last major confrontation between college and church was the controversy about creation and evolution in the late1980s. Why the lull after that conflict? I surmise several reasons. First, there may have been a case of battle fatigue. The issues had been debated for ten years, neither side seemed ready to make concessions, and all that could be said had been spoken (and written). Second, in the CRC the matter of women in ecclesiastical office became the next skirmish. Synod 1992 received two overtures against Calvin College's "evolutionary" views, but forty-three against women in office. Since the college was not particularly associated with the "women's issue," the school was not in the line of fire.

4 p. 28.

Most importantly, the CRC changed substantially after 1992. About 40,000 members (12-13 percent) left the denomination, some from the left wing of the church, but most from the right wing—the source for most of the criticism against Calvin. (Many of these members were originally in independent congregations, but since 1998 most have joined in the new United Reformed Church). The editors and writers of the two most vociferous magazines (*Christian Renewal* and *Outlook*) nearly all left the CRC. The departure of those leaders and members in effect removed them from Calvin's constituency. Since they were no longer in the CRC, for them Calvin was no longer "our school." This change did not mean that the remaining constituency approved of all that Calvin College stood for, but there was a closer "fit" between church and college than in the 1980s. Just as the denomination has been less torn by controversy, so the relationship between church and school has been more congenial.

As the church and the college begin the twenty-first century, they must continue to evaluate and calibrate their relationship, just as they did in the past. Whereas students from outside the CRC were once looked upon with suspicion, today they are welcomed for their contribution to a more comprehensive mosaic. Whereas the board at one time consisted of CRC ministers, today men and women from other church bodies are welcomed for their insight. This greater openness toward students and trustees from other church traditions is, significantly, not extended to faculty. And it may well be that church and school have to face that issue in the years to come. Although the question has not been deliberated in any synodical report or discussion, it has surfaced at the college. For example, a "Calvin College Employees Survey" of May, 1998, indicated that 35 percent of the faculty considered the requirement of faculty CRC church membership inappropriate, and during 1998 and 1999 the "Calvin-Matters" listserv dealt with the issue very intensely. Let me sketch briefly the contours of this crucial discussion.

On November 30, 1999, the Professional Status Committee (at the request of the Multicultural Affairs Committee) organized a symposium to discuss three requirements for faculty employment: being (or becoming) a member of the CRC; sending one's children to a Christian school; and signing the Form of Subscription, thereby affirming agreement with the CRC's creeds. The last requirement has not caused noticeable dissension, but the first two have. Four papers were prepared and circulated in preparation for the meeting, and the discussion at the symposium was far-ranging, often profound, and passionate.

I will not review all the pro and con arguments here; the papers prepared for the symposium present those arguments in detail and with finesse. What is significant for us here are the following questions: What would be the foundational implications if the requirements of CRC membership and Christian education for children were no longer in force? Would Calvin College maintain a meaningful relationship with the CRC? Would the college maintain its educational vision and confessional integrity? Would the college be in a better position to fulfill its aim of becoming a genuinely diverse community?

Those who want to maintain the requirements argue that the denominational tie would be greatly weakened by the abrogation. If, for example, the CRC membership of faculty would be 50 percent by 2026 (the college's sesquicentennial), the influence of the church would be dramatically reduced. This weakening of the church's influence would in turn reduce the Reformed, Calvinistic/Kuyperian underpinnings of the school. The examples cited by George Marsden in *The Soul of the American University*, and by James Burtchaell in *The Dying of the Light,* it is argued, should serve as grim warnings about the demise of the Christian heritage if church and school continue to loosen their ties. Earlier, President Diekema, although he did favor a wider choice in church membership and in school attendance, also sounded a note of restraint: "These changes represent a significant step forward in facilitating Calvin's intent to become a more multicultural community. This is one area in which we must move very cautiously and deliberately, because to open tenure positions to faculty members not committed to a Reformed theology and a Christian philosophy of education runs an extremely high risk of altering radically the nature and character of Calvin College."[5]

Those who favor loosening these requirements suggest that fidelity to the Reformed tradition should not be determined by membership in the CRC, which is still largely a Dutch and white community. Recognizing the wider Reformed tradition, especially in Presbyterianism, would greatly broaden the base of Calvin College without sacrificing its theological underpinnings. So with the Christian school requirement. One can identify with the college's educational aims without sending one's own children to a particular Christian school. Interestingly, the document, *An Expanded Statement of Mission*, although it argues strongly for continued affiliation with the CRC, opens the door to a wider vision:

> *To place oneself confessionally in the Reformed tradition is far more than to place oneself in a particular church or denomination or even mode of worship.* The uniqueness of the Reformed understanding of the institutional church inheres in its assertion that the church is a living organism comprised of believers with Christ as their head. As we form alliances with other expressions of the Christian faith, we do so as a living body of God's agency, knit together with other believers on the basis of our common confession.[6]

The authors of the document probably did not have in mind faculty requirements, but it seems to me that this avowal could be applied to faculty hiring.

This ongoing discussion is very significant, because it encompasses the question we have seen over and over again in this study: How

[5] "President's Report to the BOT," May 12-14, 1994, p. 3.
[6] p. 19 (italics added).

can Calvin College become a more open, a more comprehensive, a more inclusive community, while at the same time retaining its confessional integrity and its theological traditions?

Let me close with some insights from George Marsden, from a significant review essay of James Burtchaell's *Dying of the Light.*[7] Marsden agrees with many of Burtchaell's conclusions about the bleak history of Christian colleges and the current drift of many colleges into secularism. But Marsden rightly observes that Burtchaell's view is unduly deterministic, in that he offers virtually no hope for any school. For Marsden, however, such a drift is not inevitable for all Christian colleges, even though the dangers are real. How then is a school to maintain a "substantive Christian character"? It is not to be found in a certain form of church control or "with the specifics of a given church tradition." Rather, it is "how that tradition thinks of itself in relationship to the cultural mainstream." Marsden continues:

> Evangelical and confessional Protestant colleges today still retain a heritage of suspicion of the cultural and academic mainstream. At the same time they are increasingly becoming successful and accepted and may well aspire to greater success, acceptance, and influence. When that corner is turned the game is up, and their opening up and improvements in academic levels will be evidences that they are on the trajectory that Burtchaell describes. On the other hand, if they can retain the sense of tension with the mainstream culture, the sense that their most essential loyalties are to a city that is alien to the cities of the world, then they can retain their identity for a long time."[8]

Although Marsden does not mention Calvin College by name, much of what he says applies to Calvin. The college has become successful and influential. One can be very grateful for that success,

[7] *Christian Scholar's Review*, 29, 1 (Fall, 1999): 177-81.
[8] Pp. 180-81.

but the success of academic achievements or corporate gifts has built-in dangers. Calvin has also had a history of testing the spirits, of critiquing socialism and capitalism, the entertainment industry and racism, violence and consumerism. It is crucial for the college to continue to teach and practice kingdom values that are often at odds with the gods of the age.

I trust that Calvin College will do so, and I think that its covenant with the Christian Reformed Church will enhance its mission.

Works Cited

A number of additional titles on the background of Christian higher education and on the history of the Christian Reformed Church are listed in chapter 1, footnote 1, and chapter 2, footnote 1.

"An Expanded Statement of the Mission of Calvin College." Grand Rapids: Calvin College, 1996.

Association of Christian Reformed Laymen. *Bulletin*, October 1968-April 1981.

"Bananer Perpetrators Confess 25 Years Later." *Banner*, April 24, 1995 (2, 19-23).

Beets, Henry. *De Christelijke Gereformeerde Kerk in Noord Amerika.* Grand Rapids: Grand Rapids Printing Co., 1918.

———. "What's the Matter with Calvin?" *Banner*, November 1, 1921 (724-25).

Berkhof, Louis. "Our School's Reason for Existence and the Preservation Thereof." In *Semi-Centennial Volume, Theological School and Calvin College.* Grand Rapids: Calvin College, 1926 (114-143).

Bratt, James D. *Dutch Calvinism in Modern America: A History of a Conservative Subculture.* Grand Rapids: Eerdmans, 1984.

——— "Lammert J. Hulst: The Pastor as Leader in an Immigrant Community." In *The Dutch-American Experience: Essays in Honor of Robert P. Swierenga,* edited by Hans Krabendam and Larry Wagenaar. Amsterdam: VU Uitgeverij, 2000 (209-21).

Bratt, James D., and Ronald A. Wells. "Piety and Progress." In *Keeping Faith: Embracing the Tensions in Christian Higher Education.* Grand Rapids: Eerdmans, 1996 (20-46).

Bube, Richard H. "Review." *Perspectives: Journal of the American Scientific Affiliation* 38, 3 (September 1986): 215.

Burtchaell, James T. *The Dying of the Light: The Disengagement of Colleges and Universities from their Christian Churches.* Grand Rapids: Eerdmans, 1998.

Calvin College. Board of Trustees Minutes. Calvin College Archives.

———. *Chimes* [student weekly newspaper].

———. Presidents' Reports to the Board of Trustees. Calvin College Archives.

———. *Prism* [student annual].

———. *Year Book* [later: *Catalog*].

Christian Reformed Church. *Acts of Synod* 1857-. Grand Rapids: Christian Reformed Church in North America.

———. *Yearbook* [early dates: *Jaarboekje*] 1875-. Grand Rapids: Christian Reformed Church in North America.

"Confronting the Creation Issue." *Calvin Spark*, September, 1988 (20-24).

De Conde, Alexander. *Student Activism: Town and Gown in Historical Perspective.* New York: Scribner, 1971.

De Koster, Lester. "An Open Letter from Prof. De Koster to President of Calvin College." *Banner,* November 18, 1960 (22).

———. "Calvin Teacher Protests Against NAE's Commendation of 'The Road Ahead.'" *Banner*, August 18, 1950 (1020).

———. "*The Fourth Day*: A Critical Evaluation." *Christian Renewal,* March 23, 1987 (7).

Diekema, Anthony J. *Academic Freedom and Christian Scholarship.* Grand Rapids: Eerdmans, 2000.

———. Papers. Calvin College Archives.

Estep, James. "Faith as the Transformation of Learning." *Christian Education Journal*, 2NS (1998):59-76.

Gunneman, Louis H. *The Shaping of the United Church of Christ.* Cleveland: United Church Press, 1999.

Hart, Hendrik. "AACS in the CRC—Response." *Reformed Journal*, March, 1975 (25-28).

Hughes, Richard, and William Adrian, eds. *Models for Christian Higher Education.* Grand Rapids: Eerdmans, 1997.

Huissen, C. "Sunday Entertainment." *Torch and Trumpet*, February, 1962 (4).

Hultink, John. "Dear Calvin College Student." *Christian Renewal*, September 7, 1987 (12).

———. "What Are We to Do with Adam and Eve?" *Christian Renewal,* March 4, 1985 (8).

Kennedy, Earl Wm. "The Summer of Dominie Winter's Discontent: The Americanization of a Dutch Reformed Seceder." In *The Dutch-American Experience: Essays in Honor of Robert P. Swierenga,* edited by Hans Krabendam and Larry Wagenaar. Amsterdam: VU Uitgeverij, 2000 (223-41).

Koops, Ralph. "Twenty-five Years in Canada." *Banner*, February 21 (10-11), February 28 (16- 17), March 14 (22-23), 1975.

Krabbendam, Hans and Larry Wagenaar, eds. *The Dutch-American Experience: Essays in Honor of Robert P. Swierenga.* Amsterdam: VU Uitgeverij, 2000.

Kuiper, B. K. *The Proposed Calvinistic College at Grand Rapids.* Grand Rapids: Sevensma, 1903.

Kuiper, H. J. "Sodom and Gomorrah." *Banner,* December 12, 1947 (1380).

———. "Some Observations on Flynn's 'The Road Ahead.'" *Banner,* Aug. 25, 1950 (1028-29).

Kuiper, Klaas. "Aan Mijn Vriend." *De Wachter*, April 8, 1903 (2).

———. "Editorial." *De Wachter*, September 14, 1898 (3).

———. "Een Lang Gevoelde Behoefte." *De Wachter*, September16, 1914 (3).

———. "Meer utgebreid lager onderwijs." *De Wachter*, October 11, 1893 (1).

Kuyper, Abraham. *Publiek Vermaak*. Amsterdam: Drukkerij de Standaard, 1880.

———. *Souvereiniteit in Eigen Kring*. Amsterdam: Kruyt, 1880.

Kuyvenhoven, Andrew. "From Sabbath to Sunday." *Banner*, Sept. 26, 1983 (7-8).

Larson, David. "Evangelical Christian Higher Education, Culture, and Social Conflict." Ph.D. diss., Loyola University of Chicago, 1992.

Marsden, George M. "Review of *Dying of the Light*." *Christian Scholar's Review*, 29, 1 (Fall, 1999): 177-81.

———. *The Soul of the American University*. New York: Oxford, 1994.

Marsden, George M., Clarence Menninga, and Davis A. Young. "An open letter to the readers of *Christian Renewal*." *Christian Renewal*, May 20, 1985 (6).

Newman, Robert. "Review." *Westminster Journal* 48, 2 (Fall. 1986): 410-12.

One Hundred Years in the New World. Grand Rapids: Centennial Committee of the Christian Reformed Church, 1957.

Parsonage, Robert Rue, ed. *Church Related Higher Education*. Valley Forge, Penn.: Judson Press, 1978.

Pekelder, Bernard. "The Role of the Board of Trustees in Operating a Church-related College: A Case Study." Master's thesis, Northwestern University, 1965.

Peters, Leo. "Calvin Teaches Biblical Creation Is False." *Christian Renewal*, April 11, 1988 (5).

Plantinga, Alvin. "When Faith and Reason Clash." *Christian Scholar's Review* 21, 1 (September 1991): 8-32.

Ringenberg, William C. *The Christian College: A History of Protestant Higher Education in America*. Grand Rapids: Eerdmans, 1984.

Romanowski, William. "John Calvin Meets the Creature from the Black Lagoon: The Christian Reformed Church and the Movies 1928-1966." *Christian Scholar's Review* 25, 1, (1995): 47-62.

Rozema, Bob. "Creation and Geology." *Banner*, November 12, 1984 (10-12).

Runner, H. Evan. "Het Roer Om." *Torch and Trumpet,* April, 1953 (1-4).

Ryskamp, Henry J. *Offering Hearts, Shaping Lives: A History of Calvin College 1876-1966.* Grand Rapids: Calvin College, 2000.

Schepers, J. "Een College." *De Wachter*, March 4, 1896 (2).

Schoolland, J. B. *Living and Striving: the Emerging Pattern of My Life.* Chino, Calif.: Christian Printing Service, 1999.

Seerveld, Calvin. "Perspective for Our Christian Colleges." *Christianity Today*, September 13, 1963 (9-11).

Semi-Centennial Volume, Theological School and Calvin College 1876-1926. Grand Rapids: Theological School and Calvin College, 1926.

"Special Supplement on the Far Right." *Reformed Journal*, January 1965 (11-31).

Spoelhof, William. Correspondence. Calvin College Archives

———. "Open Letter from Dr. William Spoelhof to the Editor." *Banner*, June 26, 1970 (19).

———."Reply by President Spoelhof." *Banner*, November 18, 1960 (11).

Stob, George. "The Christian Reformed Church and her Schools." Th.D. diss., Princeton Theological Seminary, 1955.

Stob, Henry. "The Mind of the Church." *Reformed Journal*, March (3-6), April (4-9), July-August (3-6), October (13-17), 1957.

———. *Summoning Up Remembrance.* Grand Rapids: Eerdmans, 1995.

Swets, Seymour. *Fifty Years of Music at Calvin College.* Grand Rapids: Eerdmans, 1973.

Swierenga, Robert P. and Elton J. Bruins. *Family Quarrels in the Dutch Reformed Churches in the Nineteenth Century.* Grand Rapids: Eerdmans, 1999.

Ten Hoor, F. M. "De College en de Kerk." *Gereformeerde Amerikaan,* 14, 1-4 (January-April, 1910): 25-40, 89-95, 149-59, 209-16.

Timmerman, John J. *Promises to Keep: A Centennial History of Calvin College.* Grand Rapids: Eerdmans, 1976.

Tuininga, Jelle. "A Case of Misplaced Loyalty." *Christian Renewal,* August 10, 1987 (2, 17).

Turner, James C. "Something to be Reckoned With: The Evangelical Mind Awakens." *Commonweal,* January 15, 1999 (11-13).

Van Dellen, Izerd. "Het Karakter van ons Volk naar Schaduw-en Lichtzijden." In *Gedenkboek van het Vijftigjarig Jubileum de Christelijke Gereformeerde Kerk.* 2nd ed. Grand Rapids: Semi-Centennial Committee, 1907 (191-209).

Van Mouwerink, John. "Objects to Political Activity at Calvin in Recent Campaign." *Banner,* November 18, 1960 (22).

Van Till, Howard J. *The Fourth Day: What the Bible and the Heavens Are Telling Us about the Creation.* Grand Rapids: Eerdmans, 1986.

———. "When Faith and Reason Cooperate." *Christian Scholar's Review* 21, 1 (September 1991): 33-45.

Van Till, Howard J., Davis A. Young, and Clarence Menninga. *Science Held Hostage.* Downers Grove, IL: InterVarsity Press, 1988.

Van Wylen, Gordon. *Vision for a Christian College.* Grand Rapids: Eerdmans, 1988.

Vande Kieft, J. M. "The Sunday Newspaper." *Banner,* August 8, 1941 (728).

Vander Goot, Henry. "From Illusion to Restriction." Grand Rapids: Calvin College, 1989.

Vander Ploeg, John. "Do We Just Laugh This Off?" *Banner,* June 19, 1970 (8-11).

Vander Stelt, John. "Calvin College." *Church and Nation,* July 22, 1958 (40).

Verduin, Henry. "To Lovers of Calvin." *Banner*, November 18, 1960 (11).

Wichers, Wynand. "Inaugural Address." *Hope College Anchor*, October 14, 1931 (4-5c).

———. *A Century of Hope, 1866-1966*. Grand Rapids: Eerdmans, 1968.

Wolfe, Alan. "The Opening of the Evangelical Mind." *Atlantic Monthly*, October, 2000 (55-76).

Wolterstorff, Nicholas. "The AACS in the CRC." *Reformed Journal*, December, 1974 (9-16).

Young, Davis A. *Christianity and the Age of the Earth*. Grand Rapids: Zondervan, 1982.

Zwaanstra, Henry. *Reformed Thought and Experience in a New World*. Kampen: Kok, 1973.

Index